60 0408728 1

UNIVERS   AR
WITH   N
R O M

D1587970

The Loyalties
of Robinson Jeffers

Radcliffe Squires

Ann Arbor: The University of Michigan Press

UNIVERSITY LIBRARY
OCT
8
1957
NOTTINGHAM

Copyright © by the University of Michigan, 1956
Library of Congress Catalog Card No. 56–11031

c

Sonnet X from "The Truce and the Peace" from *Roan Stallion, Tamar and Other Poems* by Robinson Jeffers; "Haunted Country" from *Roan Stallion, Tamar and Other Poems* by Robinson Jeffers; copyright renewed 1953 by Robinson Jeffers

"Love the Wild Swan" from *Solstice and Other Poems* by Robinson Jeffers, copyright 1935 by Modern Library, Inc.

"Self-Criticism in February" from *Such Counsels You Gave to Me* by Robinson Jeffers, copyright 1937 by Random House, Inc. Reprinted by permission of Random House, Inc.

Permission to quote from *Flagons and Apples* and *Californians* from Robinson Jeffers

Printed in the United States of America
by George McKibbin & Son

To Brewster Ghiselin

who, come to think of it,

is just the opposite of the man from Porlock

12·68·04

                . . . but naught
There is more goodly than to hold the high
Serene plateaus, well fortressed by the wise,
Whence thou may'st look below on other men
And see them ev'rywhere wand'ring, all dispersed
In their lone seeking for the road of life;
Rivals in genius, or emulous in rank,
Pressing through days and nights with hugest toil
For summits of power and mastery of the world.
O wretched minds of men! O blinded hearts!
In how great perils, in what darks of life
Are spent the human years, however brief!

    —Lucretius, *De Rerum Natura*
      (translated by William Ellery Leonard)

    Orestes walked in the clear dawn; men say
      that a serpent
Killed him in high Arcadia. But young or old,
      few years or many, signified less than nothing
To him who had climbed the tower beyond time,
      consciously, and cast humanity, entered
      the earlier fountain.

    —Robinson Jeffers, *The Tower Beyond Tragedy*

Preface

Advantage and disadvantage minister to the study of a poet whose reputation within a relatively short time has risen very high and fallen very low. One is encouraged to seek new insights, to be skeptical of established opinion, to start, as it were, anew. But one is also obliged to quarrel with others whose evaluations have petrified as final judgments. I have had thus to differ with some whose brilliance and justice have in certain respects helped to shape my opinions.

But if I quarrel, I do not entertain the naïve assumption that I can seize the reins of criticism and reverse present opinions. Jeffers is an uneven writer, and in this century the temptation will be to judge him by his inferior rather than his best work. It is difficult, furthermore, to "place" him. His faith in direct statement and moralistic commentary suggests a traditionalism. His poetic method is heterodox without being "modern," while his concepts at the present moment seem hackneyed beyond salvage. Time's disengagement will be needed to evaluate and re-evaluate his philosophy and relate what of it remains valid to the larger "truths" of human history. Nevertheless, one thing is clear to me at the present: Jeffers' effort is major. Almost alone among contemporaries he has believed wholeheartedly that poetry cannot survive in a vacuum. Almost alone he has believed that poetry can assimilate and reconstruct in a recognizably dramatic form the peculiar disunity and disloyalty of modern man.

There have been other studies of Robinson Jeffers. Most of these are of dubious worth, but two are excellent. Lawrence Clark Powell's *Robinson Jeffers,* begun as a doctoral dissertation at the University of Dijon in 1932 and revised in 1934 and 1940, constitutes a satisfying introduction to the primary elements of Jeffers' poetry. I have drawn freely on his findings, and many of the theses which I discuss in detail developed from intimations in Powell's book. I also find S. S. Alberts' *A Bibliography of the Works of Robinson Jeffers* (1933) an indispensable aid, remarkable not alone for accuracy but also for primary source materials not otherwise accessible.

George Sterling's *Robinson Jeffers, the Man and the Artist* (1926), the first extensive appraisal of Jeffers, is fustian. Louis Adamic's *Robinson Jeffers, a Portrait* (1929) is an interesting but brief sketch of Jeffers' personality and the implications of his work. Still, Adamic's booklet along with Edith Greenan's short volume, *Of Una Jeffers* (1939), offers a fairly detailed and useful portrait of the poet. Other details of a similar sort are contained in Melba Berry Bennett's *Robinson Jeffers and the Sea* (1936), but the book is largely devoted to a compilation of passages which mention the ocean. Perhaps the most ambitious critical treatment to date is Rudolph Gilbert's *Shine, Perishing Republic* (1936). Yet, like Sterling's pamphlet, it suffers from excessive adulation, and it is put together with little regard for accuracy.

In my own study I have assumed that at least to some extent Jeffers' present reputation reflects a misapprehension of his philosophical and artistic position. I have accordingly sought to construct a cosmography from both his poetry and intellectual background. In this sense, my treatment is not primarily critical, although I have attempted to indicate the direction which I believe sympathetic criticism may justifiably take. As to the rest of the study: I have tried to examine the relationship of Jeffers' poetry to his temperament, then to philosophy and science, and finally to the work of other writers, some of whom, such as D. H. Lawrence and Walt Whitman, naturally suggest themselves, and some whose presence may surprise and outrage.

But I wish to caution that I do not advance these comparative treatments as studies in "influence." They are rather studies in literary geography: a description of terrain, a definition of boundaries. As for the position of Jeffers' work in this geography, I have desired to do no more than suggest that there is a broad plain between vast mountains and that somewhere through the plain runs a path.

My debts are many. The heaviest I owe to Howard Mumford Jones and Albert J. Guérard, Jr., who encouraged, advised, and helped me across slippery spots. I am also indebted for information to Lawrence Clark Powell. Less formally, but not less importantly, I received valuable hints from John Ciardi, Richard Eberhart, Edwin Honig, Warner Rice, and Richard Wilbur.

To Professor John Holmes of Tufts University I am obliged not only for advice but equally for placing at my disposal a copy of an address Jeffers delivered at Harvard University on March 3, 1941. I am also grateful for the perennial courtesies of staffs of the libraries at Harvard University and the University of Michigan, and of the Boston Athenaeum. And I owe much to a generous grant from the Horace H. Rackham School of Graduate Studies of the University of Michigan. Finally and most profoundly, I am indebted to a certain lady, with whom I first read the poetry of Robinson Jeffers.

R.S.

Contents

The Loyalties of Robinson Jeffers

Introduction

IT HAS BEEN the fate of Robinson Jeffers to write beyond the time which stimulated his unique expression, with the result that after an enthusiastic reception in the 1920's he has in the past fifteen years been largely forgotten. The unreasoned intensity of Jeffers' earliest admirers has perhaps been as unfortunate for his present critical reputation as the later objections of his detractors. The phrases of his discoverers, James Rorty, Mark Van Doren, and Babette Deutsch, were those usually reserved for Shakespeare, and it was inevitable that they would eventually need revision. The most shameless of his praisers was George Sterling who declared, "What men will say of Robinson Jeffers in a hundred years I wish to say now, despite the attitude of the envious, the ungenerous and the blind." And what did Sterling wish to say? Merely that as splendid as the Elizabethan dramatists undoubtedly were, one has to "go back to Aeschylus to find the match" of Jeffers' *The Tower Beyond Tragedy*.[1]

While the praise of these first admirers was wild, its

intensity is perhaps to be comprehended as religious. In an era of bathtub gin, spangled flappers, and economic frivolity, Jeffers' attack on man was chastening. Benjamin De Casseres, one of the first leaders of the Jeffers cult, in telling about his introduction to *Tamar* and *Roan Stallion,* explained that he had been employed by a cinema company as a writer; his life, he felt, was little more than a procession of "Rotarians, mystical fakirs and real estate peddlers." He found his exposure to Jeffers "comparable to my first discovery of Shelley . . . A great tragic poet, a genius of the first magnitude had swum into my ken. It was cerebral emotion . . . that only the few will understand."[2] De Casseres' experience is not greatly different from Miss Deutsch's feeling that she now knew how Keats felt "on first looking into Chapman's Homer." A similar awe colors the first review of Jeffers in *Poetry: A Magazine of Verse:*

Here was writing that seemed to spring from genius of a deep poetic compulsion, writing that had what one rarely finds in contemporary poetry—genuine passion. Here, page upon page, was a nuggeted ruggedness of imagery. Here was magnificent rhythm, responsive to the spur and rein of the thought riding it. And here were a beauty and vigor and objective immediacy of phrase—prolific, seemingly unpremeditated, yet restrained—which I dared to think unsurpassed by any other poet writing today in English.[3]

If Jeffers' poetry in the 1920's castigated a society whose feeling of guilt demanded the castigation, the whip seemed excessive when an economic depression descended. People felt that they were sufficiently chastened by the collapse of the stock market. Literature became socially and politically conscious, and a form of criticism arose to accompany it.

Jeffers' poetry was of interest to the Marxist critic for only one reason: his insistence that Western culture was becoming decadent. Such is the interest evinced by V. F. Calverton, who was happy enough to agree with Jeffers about decadence (although scarcely from the same premises and not to the same degree) and even happier to find Jeffers himself an evidence of decline.[4]

Along with the Marxists emerged the "anti-fascists" whose concerns were social without being Marxian and Christian without being religious. Halford E. Luccock, though admitting that he did not feel qualified to thread his way through Jeffers' poetry, still felt qualified to analyze it:

. . . [He] acclaims the superman, rejects the Christian God, the Christian and humanitarian scale of values. He has incidental criticism of the devastation which the pursuit of money has brought about in life. But when one asks to what Jeffers' glorification of violence leads, the familiar outlines of fascism appear, including faith in a strong man, a "Fuehrer" inhibited by no weakening ethical superstitions. Surely Jeffers is a supreme example of Walter Lippmann's phrase, "trading a majestic faith for a trivial illusion."[5]

Others in the touchy times of the late 1930's found Jeffers, who in *The Women at Point Sur* (1927) argues specifically against the Nietzschean ideals, an exponent of the superman. And they found him the antichrist, while ignoring that he is probably the most deeply religious of all twentieth-century American poets. The Marxian and religious-social attacks jelled into a kind of standard opinion in the pronouncements of *Time* magazine, which in 1937 told its broad public that Jeffers was irretrievably split between "the aging prophet still hell-bent on emitting clouds of sulphur and smoke, and the poet simultaneously becoming more and more corner-loving and mealy-eyed."[6] If *Time's* denigrations wanted dignity, they were nevertheless much like those of more nearly literate organs and their critics who, as Jeffers' books continued to appear with surprising regularity in the 1930's, reversed the earlier opinion of him as the "great" tragic poet and substituted the opinion of him as the hysterical charlatan.

John Gould Fletcher was content in 1934 with merely weakening Jeffers' position, finding that "his poems tend to get less and less interesting as he is obliged, by the tenets of his own inhuman creed, to make use in every poem of characters with strong streaks of neurotic obsession; or else to write pompous and inflated absurdity . . ." Despite this large difficulty, however, Fletcher still felt that:

. . . he will always be a valuable, an important poet, [though] he will never achieve that apparently inevitable fusion of earthly and eternal interests which is what the world demands from its great poets. Of the qualities that go to make up a supreme poet: a Homer, a Shakespeare, a Milton, an Aeschylus, or a Goethe, he possesses only *some*.[7]

It is clear that Fletcher did not belong to the Jeffers cult, yet his words seem to me sensitive, pertinent, and highly laudatory. His imputation of repetitiousness prefigured the more serious doubts of Robert Penn Warren, who, while he could still write in 1937 that Jeffers was an "established poet," felt that *Solstice* ". . . is like nothing so much as an ether dream Jeffers might have about some of his own poetry. . . . In relation to the better of the earlier narratives the present one is repetition without direction."[8]

To the complaint (entirely justified) of self-imitation one may add the accusation first leveled by H. H. Waggoner that Jeffers' characters "who dominate the poems are ultimate expressions of what certain trends in materialistic science have to say about man."[9] Professor Waggoner's observation was repeated by Delmore Schwartz, who raised the list of complaints to include Jeffers' "breaches of consistency in the rhythm."[10] Clearly, this brings up the problem of form and in turn the problem of Jeffers' relationship to the "new critics," who remained aloof from the Marxists by insisting that poetry had no social effect or value and therefore no historical bearings except insofar as literature and esthetics yield a history.

The new criticism has been successful mainly in its explication of the complex, polydirectional lyric: the lyrics of Donne or of the contemporary neo-metaphysicals. But its success is the measure of its failure, for the new criticism has not been at any time comfortable in treating the epical creation. For this reason, the new critics have tended to sacrifice the Milton to the Donne, or—what is perhaps only fantastic—to suggest that Milton, after all, insofar as he is a good poet, is also a metaphysical, a "difficult" poet. Furthermore, since they deal primarily with glyptic verse, these critics have consistently turned away from traditional Nature poetry which, being descriptive and often simple, does not usually command an intricate, urbane response.

Yet this is not to say that the new critics have not performed a valuable service. If their achievement has not been large, it has been intense. At the same time, I cannot avoid suspecting that the new method leads to attenuation. An obsession with verbal ping-pong in poetry encourages a faith in a specious individuality in a given poem, and when that happens, criticism becomes a series of special opinions, rather than a set of standards. It seems also to mean that the critic becomes paralyzed by subtlety, denatured by boredom—or, alas, at an opposite extreme, dancing-mad with ingeniousness.

Jeffers' relationship with the new criticism has had two consequences. The first of these is Yvor Winters' attack of Jeffers' whole achievement,[11] an attack with a late echo in R. P. Blackmur's reference to "the flannel-mouthed inflation in the metric of Robinson Jeffers with his rugged rockgarden violence."[12] The second is probably more damaging: I refer to the silence of the new critics. This silence seems perfected in John Crowe Ransom's selection of the major and minor poets of the first fifty years of the century.[13] The selection does not include or even obliquely mention Jeffers, who between the years 1928 and 1941 occupied a "position as a poet among his contemporaries . . . that can almost be compared with Victor Hugo's eminence in France of the mid-nineteenth century."[14]

Of course, the silence of these critics is understandable; they have devoted themselves to a real enough need in contemporary literature, the need of detailed exegesis of highly allusive and difficult poetry. Jeffers' poetry presents some difficulties, but it is in the main poetry of direct statement. Yet even if Jeffers were serving up a pastiche of metaphysical conceits and French symbolism, it seems unlikely that the "esthetic" critics would feel moved to enthusiasm for his sprawling, often careless narratives. The poems need critical re-examination, but the need centers in their philosophical texture, in the relationship of idea to idea rather than the relationship of word to word, nuance to nuance.

Other factors have probably contributed to neglect of Jeffers. For one thing, there is his isolation from the cliques of poets who stalk the pages of the little magazines, reviewing the books of their friends—and of their enemies. In the first burst of rising reputation, Jeffers, it is true, reviewed the books of those poets who had brought his work to the attention of the public: James Rorty, Miss Deutsch, and Mark Van Doren. His reviews, although biased by his own preconceptions, are interesting, but it would appear that he did not choose to be a reviewer, for his reviews cease with his having "paid back" those who had been the first friends of his work.

One may add a final reason for the near-oblivion: the fact that Jeffers has had no successful imitators. True, John Evans wrote a silly novel about incest in the California hills (*Shadows Flying,* 1936), dedicating it to "You and Robin, Una"; and Walter Van Tilburg Clark, who wrote a starry-eyed master's thesis on Jeffers, has shown a preoccupation with Jeffers' themes. But the only important and certainly the most unhappy consequence of an attempt to ape Jeffers may be found in Edna St. Vincent Millay's later work, where the harp which had twanged merrily, if somewhat thinly, seems to break under the themes of social decline and despair. Still, if Jeffers has not been successfully imitated, other poets who have tried to write narrative verse have been hard put to avoid wandering into Jeffers' music and rhetoric. I think the reason for this is simply that Jeffers found a language and a metric appropriate to his age and his intent.

In retrospect Jeffers' present reputation is contained within the beautiful symmetry of a completed irony. The virtues which the earlier reception proclaimed were his sense of restrained tragedy, his form and metrical accomplishment. The faults which later criticism has found are those of hysteria, formlessness and dubious metrics. Still, most critics have permitted him to retain one virtue, that of "power." A recent review in *Poetry* observes:

. . . there are parts of *The Double Axe* which isolated alike from the action and the convictions which underly the work, possess an enormous power. They are, almost exclusively, those sections in which the sheer violence and magnificence of Mr. Jeffers' invective make themselves felt. *Saeva indignatio* is, of itself, a compelling species of writing, and it is possible to admire the virtuosity of Mr. Jeffers at this art while forgetting, at the moment, the object of his attack.[15]

Savage indignation is a fit description of Jeffers' power, but it is misleading as well as absurd to suppose that his indignation (or his power) can or should be "isolated alike from the action and the convictions which underly the work" or from "the object of his attack." That is to ask us to read *Gulliver's Travels* as an angry fairy tale without relevance to mankind. The significant implication here, as elsewhere, is that Jeffers' central position, his doctrine of Inhumanism, has been misinterpreted by being partly, but not wholly, understood.

Jeffers' literary reputation has ebbed steadily since 1935, and he is now being dropped from anthologies and consigned to the ranks of those who present only "historical" interest. One of the late histories of American poetry dismisses him with one sentence: "Later, the isolated Robinson Jeffers was to begin to construct a peculiar misanthropic world through a series of dramatic poems acted out against a wild background of California coastline."[16] Whether the dismissal is fair or unfair may not be decided in the near future, but the fact that Jeffers now occupies a vague place in the history of American literature justifies an effort to discover his world.

I

The Destroying Prodigal

1

JOHN ROBINSON JEFFERS was born in 1887 at Pittsburgh, Pennsylvania, the son of Dr. William Hamilton Jeffers and Annie Robinson Tuttle Jeffers. Of Scotch-Irish-English ancestry, Dr. Jeffers, who held the chair of Old Testament Literature and Exegesis at Western Theological Seminary, had met Annie Tuttle, who was twenty-three years younger than he, while visiting a small Presbyterian church where she was organist. One other child, a son Hamilton, was born in 1894.

Jeffers' education was scattered. He attended private schools in Pennsylvania and a boarding school in Switzerland; he learned, we are told, "to think in Italian, French and German."[1] His interest in poetry flowered when in Switzerland at the age of fourteen or fifteen he got hold of the poems of Thomas Campbell and Dante Gabriel Rossetti. He writes:

Neither name meant anything to my mind; nor did Campbell's poetry; but no lines of print will ever intoxicate as Ros-

setti's rather florid verses did, from *The Blessed Damozel* to the
least last sonnet. I wonder why was that? How had Long-
fellow's *Hiawatha,* or Horace or La Fontaine, or association
football and the Swiss lakes, conditioned my mind to thrill to
Rossetti?

My pleasure was pure; I was never a critical reader . . .
now if I should ever wonder about the uses of poetry, I have
only to remember that year's experience. . . . Later came *The
Wind among the Reeds,* and Shelley, and Tennyson's *Alcaics*
and *Boadicea,* doubtful imitations of classical meter but sonorous
as the beat of surf; when I grew older came Milton and Marlowe and many another; normal and reasonable raptures; but
never again the passionate springtime that Rossetti (of all
authors!) made me live.[2]

Jeffers returned from Switzerland in 1902 and completed a sophomore year at the University of Pittsburgh. In
the following year his father's health required the removal
of the family to a kindlier climate. They settled in Pasadena, California, and Jeffers entered Occidental College,
receiving his B.A. degree two years later at the age of
eighteen. While at Occidental he edited the college literary
magazine, wrote verses, and fell in love with the brilliant
and beautiful Mrs. Una Call Kuster. In 1913 she became his
wife, but in the meantime, the fact that she had a husband,
a young lawyer known as "Teddy," was a source of distress
to both of them. Jeffers' parents, in an effort, one supposes,
to discourage his relationship with a married woman two
years his senior, took him to Europe in 1907. Once again in
Switzerland, he contemplated studying at the University of
Zurich. Instead "he returned . . . to Los Angeles, and en-
rolled in the College of Medicine at the University of South-

ern California. He had no intention of becoming a physician, but was interested in medicine as a science."[3]

In 1910 he abandoned medicine and with his parents moved to Seattle. Here he studied forestry at the University of Washington until 1911. But, excepting the summer spent at Hermosa Beach, he seems mostly to have pined for Mrs. Kuster. The next year, 1912, he inherited a modest legacy from a remote relative. He became financially independent and at his own expense published his first collection of verse, *Flagons and Apples,* "then returned to the University of Washington, where until the spring of 1913 he sought distraction . . . in a study of Zoology and Law, in addition to his forestry course."[4]

Mrs. Kuster was also seeking distraction at this time in Europe, or possibly she had gone abroad in order to make up her mind between her husband and Jeffers. At any rate the situation was eased by Teddy's falling in love with Edith Greenan, the woman who later was to write a book of warm reminiscences about Una. Mrs. Kuster obtained a divorce and she and Jeffers were married in Tacoma on August 2, 1913. On the eve of the wedding, Jeffers wrote rhapsodically to Mrs. Nash, at whose home he had boarded at Hermosa Beach:

My dear Mrs. Nash:

Tomorrow we'll be mailing you the announcement of our wedding, and I suppose you'll receive it at the same time as this letter. It hardly seems possible that we are really going to be married tomorrow; so great a happiness is almost incredible. But it is true. This morning we left Seattle and came to Tacoma, and this afternoon we went to the court house here and got the marriage license. My mother, as Una has told you, has been with us in Seattle for the last three weeks; she is staying with us now, and will start for California early tomorrow afternoon, soon after the ceremony is performed. We are very glad that she is going to be here to see us married, and I think that she has very much enjoyed her stay in the north. I wish you too could be here, my foster-mother.

You'll be surprised, I'm sure, to hear that Una and I intend going to Europe this winter. Una enjoys England and her English friends so much that I think it will give her great happiness to go there again and to live there for a year or two. And I shall be able to work as well there as in America—perhaps better. At any rate the experience will be helpful to me, and I look forward to it with great pleasure. We'll come back to visit California after a year, I think; but probably a good deal of our future life will be spent in England and on the Continent.

Our plan is to remain in Seattle until the middle of September; then to go to Los Angeles—and Hermosa—for almost three weeks. After that we'll go straight to Europe, stopping only for a few days in New York.

So we'll see you, Mrs. Nash, in September; and I'm looking forward with more pleasure than I can tell you to staying a fortnight in Hermosa. You have always been so good to me, and I have a son's affection for you—how anxious I am to see you and talk to you!

It is almost midnight, and I shall have to close this letter—the last I shall write before my marriage. I'll write again very soon, and more fully, about our plans and our experiences. Thank you ever so much for your sweet letter which I received yesterday morning.

Goodnight, my dear Mrs. Nash,

Robin[5]

Those familiar with Jeffers' later reserve will find the young man's ebullient expression of happiness surprising. But, if he found happiness in 1913, events were shortly to conspire against the fulfillment of his hopes. Despite his and Una's avowal to live abroad (they thought of the Aegean as well as England), Jeffers was not destined to join the ranks of American expatriates. The plans for going abroad were delayed and at length abandoned when war broke out in Europe. The war itself was shocking, and in addition the year 1914 brought two personal sorrows, the death of his infant daughter Maev and of his father. These and the war Jeffers treated together in his stilted, yet splendid ode "The Year of Mourning," printed in his second volume, *Californians* (1916). Although the deaths of "the flower first-born" and "the father-stem"—along with an intimation that civilization was also dying in the European war—overwhelmed him, there was one compensation. Unable to travel in Europe, he came with Una by "pure accident" to the Carmel coast,

. . . where for the first time in my life I could see people living—amid magnificent unspoiled scenery—essentially as they did in the Idyls or the Sagas, or in Homer's Ithaca. Here was life purged of its ephemeral accretions. Men were riding after cattle, or plowing the headland, hovered by white sea-gulls, as they have done for thousands of years, and will for thousands of years to come. Here was contemporary life that was also permanent life; and not shut from the modern world but conscious of it and related to it; capable of expressing its spirit, but unencumbered by the mass of poetically irrelevant details and complexities that make a civilization.[6]

Jeffers' twin sons, Donnan and Garth, were born in 1916, and when America entered the war, he "did not enlist in the ranks because," as Una Jeffers later wrote:

. . . we had little money and no immediate expectation of more, and our twin boys were infants. After suffering consider-

able disturbance of mind, he made various unsuccessful appli-
cations for training for a commission; he was examined for
aviation and rejected for high blood pressure. However he had
been provisionally accepted for balloon service and was awaiting
instructions when peace was declared.[7]

The war may have seemed more catastrophic to Jeffers as a
spectator than it would have had he been personally involved. Be that as it may, engrossed by the monstrous up-
heaval, he sought compensation in the most "permanent"
things he could find. He turned to building Tor House
from the Pacific granite, working with the masons on the
house; and then for five years he toiled with a primitive
hand-pulley to erect Hawk Tower. Even when happier
times came, his faith remained with the relative indestruct-
ibility of stone. On the eve of a second World War, when
he camped overnight "in the pathless gorge of Ventana
Creek" and watched the flames of the campfire flickering
across his son's face, his characteristic horror of life's im-
permanence swept over him. But the "rock wall"—that was
different.

> I shall die, and my boys
> Will live and die, our world will go on through its rapid
> agonies of change and discovery; this age will die,
> And wolves have howled in the snow around a new Beth-
> lehem: this rock will be here, grave, earnest, not pas-
> sive: the energies
> That are its atoms will still be bearing the whole mountain
> above: and I, many packed centuries ago,
> Felt its intense reality with love and wonder, this lonely
> rock.

With the publication of *Tamar* in 1924 the effect of
his conversion to a religion of lithic permanency became

clear. He had begun his long quarrel with man's deliberate separation from the somber continuity of Nature, and what angered him most was that in discarding the values of the primitive heart man seemed incapable of substituting the calm values of the civilized mind. There had been a great war, and he knew there would be another. Such a war, he felt, could not reassert the heroic values of Thermopylae (how splendid if it could!), but it could, and only would, prove the assertion of the adage, as applied to world history, that there is no fool like an old fool. And so he came to write violent "stories" about two heroes: Nature as permanence opposed to man as the perverse, ephemeral consciousness. But Jeffers' violence is not so much nostalgia for Thermopylae as it is scorn of modern man's playing the old fool: modern man with his bloody and mysterious myths gone and with his theory of ethics firmly established, yet behaving like a barbarian—like the child, instead of the adult of the age. War appears again and again in the backgrounds of the narratives as the secret, muted embodiment of a fate which, terrible as it is, may ultimately be the means of humbling the one hero (man) so as to bring him into unity with the other hero (Nature). Through this complexity of motivation, as subjectively emotional as it is objectively ideological, the reader must approach Jeffers. He must be willing to look through the violence to discover the paradoxical figure of Siva, destroyer and creator; he must trace the violence back to 1914 as Jeffers himself does, writing in 1933:

. . . there was a time in my youth when physical violence appeared more or less anachronistic. It was hope that this "old ballad-material" belonged to the past, all tragic feeling would soon be only of the mind and spirit. Unhappily that time was not normal but a rootless exception, and died nineteen years ago.[8]

While this is not the time to write a full biography, to these simple outlines of Jeffers' life it seems important to add some richness—at least to one phase, the period of his metamorphosis from the romantic young man to the re-served stone mason, hovering like his poetry about Carmel. The metamorphosis is profounder than is generally re-alized, and its relationship to his poetry, particularly to his first volumes, has not been fully recognized.

Flagons and Apples (1912) celebrates the despairs of an adolescent affair with "Helen," but, as her name sug-gests, Jeffers is addressing not one girl but the eternal femi-nine. One of the poems definitely, and two or three others probably, refer to Una, but the majority do not seem to. Amorous, freighted with flutters, accusations, and self-recriminations, the tone of the poems is dimly Shelley's. Something of Ernest Dowson also seeps in: "The shadow of an old love yesterday / Went by me on the street."

Now turning to *Californians,* one is immediately struck by changes which obviously prefigure the mature Jeffers. Most of the poems are short narratives with a re-gional bias. The forms remain traditional, but the Shel-leyan notes have yielded to stronger ones. His concept of man is, in its sweeping generality and didacticism, Words-worthian: "We grow to be what / We have loved." The diction is often reminiscent of Milton's: "... and sweet wine / Illicit he had drunk." Indeed, the general feeling in the poems is that Jeffers is struggling against the Miltonic pres-ence. The poem "Ruth Alison" begins in a style which is almost that of *Roan Stallion.* Then quite suddenly the tonality becomes Keatsian-Miltonic:

Under the awful shade immense
It runs, of immemorial redwood boughs
That downward writhe from the columnar trunks;
Trunks that by girth and noblest height, and form
Uncouth, suddenly tapering at the peak,
Recall to mind the giant world, and growths
Exorbitant, that rose from watery soil
Into the fume and rush of monstrous heavens
Ere man was born on earth . . .

Jeffers was never afterward to write so conspicuously in the shadow of Milton, but he has never entirely abandoned certain elements of the Miltonic style. It turns up in such phrases as "with speech incomprehensible" and "All will be worse confounded soon," lines published as late as 1941.

Californians contains other and more important adumbrations of the later poetry. Richard in "The Vardens" is the prodigal son who, like Hood in *Cawdor,* returns with tragic results to a hostile father. Manvil's wife in "Ruth Alison" prefigures the unfaithful wives and scheming Liliths of Jeffers' later stories. The fascination which the child in "Dorothy Atwell" has for a white horse (identified with the sea) may be taken as the work sheets for the zooerastia in *Roan Stallion.* Incest, as others have pointed out, underlies the theme of "The Three Avilas." Rather curiously, "Cauldwell's ranch" ("Cauldwell" is Tamar's family name) is mentioned in "The Mill Creek Farm." Yet, as patently embryonic as these instances are, the profounder relationship between *Californians* and Jeffers' riper utterance centers in the volume's contempt and distrust of the city, the fear of a maniacal "break-up time, when the world turns upside down, / With her sons all gone and rotted away in town."

Because *Californians* contains stylistic and ideological particles from *Flagons and Apples* while suggesting the emphasis of the mature work, it has usually been thought a "transitional" book. But when one reads the verse which the youthful Jeffers wrote and published in the Occidental College literary magazine from 1903 to 1905, one finds the nuclei of Jeffers' later attitudes as clearly as in *Californians*. Young Robin, writing of "old mother Earth," informs us that she "seems huge and almost boundless." But that "Situate / Amid the depths of space ... her greatness somewhat doth abate." How many times was the mature poet to remind man that his earth is but a small planet in the ocean of galaxies?

Similarly the budding poet in 1903 asked, "What is man that he should be proud?" And he commented:

> His place is back with the crowd,
>   His dwellings are high, and then—
>   The lonely bittern sings
>   In his ruined halls once proud,
>   And the little fox makes its den
>   Inside the dwellings of kings.

Is this not the identical spirit which pervades the narratives of historical decadence? Is not his youthful question, "What is man that he should be proud?" related to his stated intent in *The Women at Point Sur* to write "a satire of human self-importance"?

Considered as a whole, the early efforts are closer to the achievement of *Californians* than is *Flagons and Apples*. They are also cleaner and solider poems than the celebrations of "Helen." If they contain, as I believe they do, the kernel of Jeffers' mature work, and if *Flagons and*

Apples (except very rarely) does not, then one must give up the idea that *Californians* is a "transitional" work and recognize instead that it continues the mood that Jeffers has courted with only one deviation since adolescence. That one deviation is *Flagons and Apples*.

Although *Flagons and Apples* emerges as an interruption, an odd tangent in Jeffers' development, it has some importance, for it seems to document that time when he floundered most before making the choice which is responsible for the character of the greater body of his poetry. To examine the lyrics in *Flagons and Apples* closely is to find a vague record of guilt mingled with the erotic sighs. The young Jeffers bows, prostrated before a jealous God:

> O wild and cruel and occult God,
> Have mercy on thy worshipper!

And if in general he plays the part of the young lover properly, he also reveals that the objects of his adoration are a source of guilty perturbation:

> O women, will you never cease
> Weaving your spells and plotting how
> To fold me in a vile content,
> And lap me in an evil peace?
> I cannot give you pleasure now,
> Who am songless now, and impotent.

While the relation between early poems and biography is usually stronger than with mature creations, it is possible, of course, to read too much into these foolish poems, and I am not eager to make an absolute case. I suggest that there are echoes in *Flagons and Apples* of some deeper strife than the glandular wonder adolescence usually imposes. It is only sporting, too, to note that Jeffers disclaims any autobiographical basis. His "Epilogue" to the book blames the poems on the romantic scenery of California:

> For our country here at the west of things
> Is pregnant of dreams; and west of the west
> I have lived ...

No one probably ever takes this kind of recantation seriously, but it is noteworthy that this apology for his adolescent eroticism is identical with that which he makes ten years later for the sexual violence and brutality in his narratives, claiming in "Apology for Bad Dreams" that the "pain and terror" are "This coast crying out for tragedy."

Whatever one wishes to make of *Flagons and Apples,* one must face up to the fact that the Jeffers who wrote the love songs is the antithesis in most ways of the later man. The picture of Jeffers at Occidental College and at the University of Southern California is, to be sure, that of a somewhat eccentric, reserved young man—but also something of a dandy. He was in the habit of "wearing light gray peg-top trousers and a baggy coat, which then was the height of fashion," for "he belonged to the well-dressed crowd."[9] Extraordinarily handsome, he apparently attracted a number of girls, and from one of them he received letters which threw Una into fits of rage.[10] And this is especially strange: he conceived an enthusiasm for George Moore's *Confessions of a Young Man,* which he read on and off during the time he was composing *Flagons and Apples.*[11] Now, it is not difficult to account for most of Jeffers' enthusiasms— Thomas Hardy, W. H. Hudson, D. H. Lawrence, to mention a few—but George Moore seems just preposterous enough to be tantalizing. Yet it is not impossible that the decadence and dilettantism of the *Confessions* reflect a manner of life which for a time enthralled Jeffers. He may have been aware of the raffish bohemianism of the California "literary life" of Jack London, Ambrose Bierce, and George Sterling, although of these he knew only Sterling and only met him many years later. Perhaps also the gossamer abnormality, the affectation and preciosity of George Moore, along with his studied emotional license, seemed to the young Jeffers the proper accouterments for a writer. Was he tempted by the mildly charming satanism of Moore, or may he even have dreamed of duplicating the delicate nonsense of Moore's life in Paris? Whatever the truth may be, Jeffers did once write in the mood of George Moore; only once, in his only published piece of fiction, the story "Mirrors," which appeared in the August, 1913, issue of *The Smart Set,* which at that time, despite the muscularity of H. L. Mencken's and George Nathan's contributions, was still dedicated to the elegant limpness that had characterized it for a number of years. "Mirrors" is urbane and not a little *fin de siècle.*

A period of emotional involvement, uncertainty, and bohemianism is scarcely abnormal in the youth of a creative person. But there is reason to believe that for Jeffers this phase of his life was accompanied by the strongest remorse. In after-years he wrote of his "wasting on women's bodies wealth of love," and in a more worldly mood: "I was too young for my age ... and drank a good deal ..."[12] Well, perhaps, but Jeffers did not become an alcoholic. One cannot help speculating as to whether or not he felt himself to be a disappointment to his religious father. Some such feeling crops up on more than one occasion in the poetry but perhaps most strikingly in the sonnet "To His Father," published in 1924.

Christ was your lord and captain all your life,
He fails the world but you he did not fail

.   .   .   .

I Father having followed other guides
And oftener to my hurt no leader at all,
Through years nailed up like dripping panther hides
For trophies on a savage temple wall
Hardly anticipate that reverend stage
Of life, the snow-wreathed honor of extreme age.

During these "years nailed up like dripping panther hides,"
Jeffers might have become a very different kind of artist.
He might, had he followed the tangent of *Flagons and
Apples,* have decided, like a Rimbaud, to "cast on" humanity instead of casting it out. And indeed he seems to be
aware of having approached something like this as the
tenth sonnet in the sequence "The Truce and the Peace"
may testify.

All in a simple innocence I strove
To give myself away to any power,
Wasting on women's bodies wealth of love,
Worshipping every sunrise mountain tower;
Some failure mocked me still denying perfection,
Parts of me might be spended not the whole,
I sought of wine surrender and self-correction,
I failed, I could not give away my soul.
Again seeking to give myself I sought
Outward in vain through all things, out through God,
And tried all heights, all gulfs, all dreams, all thought.
I found this wisdom on the wonderful road,
The essential Me cannot be given away,
The single Eye, God cased in blood-shot clay.

This sonnet sequence marks the beginning of the maturation of Jeffers' mysticism. And a progress toward a mystical resolution was inevitable, for, partly in the face of a deeply felt experience and partly as the result of the mysteries of basic personality, he had made bluntly internecine allegiances. He loved the stormy thunder on the headland but also the deep sight of the relaxing, infinitely irenic night. He sought to preserve what he considered his own bitterly purchased stonelike reserve while he admired Una's social competence and emotional candor. He wished for peace and reason among men, yet his pulse quickened to the feral music of strife and disaster. When he most readily and scornfully rejected humanism, he most anxiously longed for his father's religious humanism. And all of these conflicts reflect his own essential conflict between death and resurrection. Critics have generally found only Jeffers' negative assertion—they have called it "nihilism." Yet the truth is that Jeffers has loved annihilation no more nor less than creation, death no more nor less than life. But loving both, he could reconcile them only in a mystical experience. If we read his poetry wisely, we gain insight into the severity, the humility, and discipline of a noble and great man's mystical solutions to problems which universally confront all men. We enter a place where the wild wind of our irrational origins turns in a ceaseless dance with the wind of our rational aspirations.

Yet Jeffers' mysticism, like all true mysticism, seeks to objectify as well as to discover the personality. His inner world is not the labyrinth of subjective emotions. It is rather the divine and terrible minotaur who waits in the final cavern of the labyrinth. The formative storm and stress in Jeffers' inner world between the years 1910 and

1918 is recorded in "The Truce and the Peace," and I judge that the important and catastrophic signification of his experience was the decision to destroy his own dandyism, the pastel romanticism of *Flagons and Apples*. He supplanted the bohemian with the stone mason. He no longer wore peg-topped trousers and the coat of fashion, but army pants, leggings, and homemade shirts, and what he came to scorn most were the values of George Moore, even though he maintained, possibly out of a wry sense of humor or even as a self-admonition, his liking for Moore's *Confessions*. As Browning turned against his *Pauline* or Goethe against his *Werther,* Jeffers turned against *Flagons and Apples*. Consciously he crushed out his adolescence and turned to writing his narratives where, if the way was labyrinthine, the goal was the minotaur. In taking this step Jeffers was pushed by his adoration of his father—and pulled by his love for his wife.

One gathers from Mrs. Greenan's account that Una had not belonged in the kind of society favored by her first husband. It was, to be sure, pleasant enough and probably exciting, but too mundane and superficial for Una's temperament. But she discovered herself in marriage with Jeffers, and it was appropriate that she should help him toward peace since she had, obviously, played a large part in his period of emotional uncertainty. In *Descent to the Dead* (1931) he reminded her of their hectic past:

> When you and I on the Palos Verdes cliff
> Found life more desperate than dear,
> And when we hawked at it on the lake by Seattle . . .

Once they were married, however, she brought him stability and purpose. Indeed, it was she who encouraged him

to work with his hands on Tor House. She also suggested
to him some of the settings and the inklings of the tales he
was to write. As Mrs. Greenan recounts, she brought him
eyes and ears. And Jeffers, as did Mrs. Greenan, found Una
"the very wildest (in the sense of the most natural) person." She came to represent for him the ideal of life: the
simple, the intense, the primitive. She is one aspect of the
symbol of the hawk in his poetry. Jeffers consciously contrasted her with his immoral heroines. In *Mara* he wrote:

> . . . Fawn a somewhat degenerate animal
> Craving love more than giving it had not been able
> To suckle her baby: she had small virgin breasts,
> And now recovered from childbirth her smooth belly
> Looked virgin too.

As he wrote this he must have been thinking of Una, who
once wrote to Mrs. Greenan: "I nursed the twins for ten
months and apparently I'm the only woman in history
who ever did."[13] Strong, beautiful, almost fierce, she was
his "pole star." She alone could inspire the stone mason to
tender lyrics—which no poet since Yeats has surpassed.

> I built her a tower when I was young—
> Sometime she will die—
> I built it with my hands, I hung
> Stones in the sky.
>
> Old but still strong I climb the stone—
> Sometime she will die—
> Climb the steep rough steps alone,
> And weep in the sky.

And in September, 1950, Una Jeffers died. As her life was
a presence in the poems from 1912 to 1950, her death will
be a presence in whatever Jeffers writes in the future.

2

The effect of Jeffers' reaction against dandyism appears in *Californians,* but it emerges full-fledged only in *Tamar* (1924) and *Roan Stallion* (1925). The change between these and *Californians* is far reaching. The regionalism has grown into an allegiance to place, but the Carmel coast of which he writes is a created world where the gothic splendors correspond less to any geography than to conditions of the imagination. The intricate verse forms have, except in a few poems which antedate *Tamar,* yielded to the long sweep of his verse paragraphs.

Between *Tamar* and *Roan Stallion* themselves there is a difference indicative of what Jeffers' future was to be. *Tamar* tells an involved story of a neurotic girl who seduces her brother and then, pregnant by him, takes another lover, a dupe, whom she intends to marry. But she seems to have fallen into the habit of incest and turns her charms next upon her aged father, who in his youth had committed incest with his sister Helen. Helen herself wanders in and out of the narrative as a ghost. Tamar's ambitions exceed mortal love, and at a séance conducted by her Aunt Stella, she experiences in one evening an astounding number of ghostly violations. Finally, with her brother, her father, and the duped lover, Tamar is cremated when the idiot, Jinny, sets the house afire, but not, unfortunately, before incident is heaped on incident and the last hiss is teased from the last, least syllable.

The contrast with *Roan Stallion* is major. Where *Tamar* is surcharged, *Roan Stallion* is sparing. As the poets Horace Gregory and Marya Zaturenska have remarked:

No narrative poem written by an American during the twentieth century is a better example of the classical rules of unity than Jeffers' "Roan Stallion": place, time, action, its characters, and its emotional temper are of one piece; and even its violent scenes of action fall with propriety within the design of the poem. If they are removed from their context, individual episodes within the poem become ridiculous, but the poem itself, like a canvas filled by the seemingly harsh and "impossible" colors of Delacroix, has its own life and its own veracity, and these are as rare in poetry as they are in painting.[14]

Taken together, *Tamar* and *Roan Stallion* reveal the double potential in Jeffers, the saga formula and the classical, the diffuse and the unified. All his later work is conceived in relationship to this artistic polarity. But he was never again to achieve the same kind of classical expression as in *Roan Stallion*. He was to write more simply than in *Tamar*, to be sure, but the crowded and episodic nature of Tamar is characteristic of even as remarkable a poem as *Cawdor* or as *The Loving Shepherdess*. Yet, if he could not wholeheartedly turn again to the classical control of *Roan Stallion*, he was able to hybridize his classical side with his undisciplined side in the narrative which achieves the greatest success, *The Double Axe* (1948). Part I of *The Double Axe* is as unified as *Roan Stallion*, whereas Part II is as diffuse and formless as *Tamar* or *The Women at Point Sur*. But Part II stands as a commentary on Part I and it takes the form of a strained, interior argument behind which the lurid lights of *Tamar* flash without dispersing the purity and intensity of the argument. Toward *The Double Axe* all of Jeffers' verse moved inexorably, and it is the result of his having been able, after years of dross, to hold the two poles of his artistic nature together. His dramas, it may be noted, display the same pattern. If one discounts his *Media,* which is contained by the architecture of Euripides, one finds that *The Tower Beyond Tragedy* and *At the Fall of an Age* correspond in their unity to *Roan Stallion,* while *Dear Judas* and *The Bowl of Blood* correspond in their disunity to *Tamar*. Also, his best drama (as poetic drama) is *At the Birth of an Age* which, like *The Double Axe,* divides into two parts: the first, an orderly, lean set of actions; the second, a purposeful disunity spun out into the searching self-analysis of the hanged God. These hybrid creations, combining his two opposed powers, along with *Roan Stallion* and his recent supernatural allegory *Hungerfield* (1952), seem to me to be Jeffers' only long works that have a chance for permanency. And not, probably, all of these. But one wonders why Jeffers could never return to the formality of *Roan Stallion*. The answer seems embedded in the relationship between *Tamar* and *Roan Stallion* and in what these two narratives stand for within Jeffers' personality.

In *Tamar* Jeffers concentrates the rays of attention on the sins of flesh until a necessary conflagration occurs. This conflagration may represent a purgation for Jeffers but it scarcely offers any solution for the depravity of man. In *Roan Stallion* there is not the same need for him to explore all the caves of sin because he has *Tamar* immediately behind him and, more importantly, he is beginning to form a solution to the problem of sin. His solution is his doctrine of Inhumanism, a term which he did not, however, use until 1948. In *Roan Stallion* the doctrine appears only incidentally; he was not certain as to the implications of "breaking out of humanity." As he became more certain, it became more necessary to stack up details of a violent nature in order to support his feeling that to live meaningfully one must withdraw from the ordinary ambitions of life. Hence his narratives tended to follow the pattern of *Tamar* where, ironically, the doctrine does not appear at all. In 1937 with *Such Counsels You Gave to Me* Jeffers tried to recapture the classical formula of *Roan Stallion,* but by that time his philosophy had so absorbed him that, even though *Such Counsels You Gave to Me* is economical, the sparse detail —in order to balance the heavy weight of his conceptual position—is exaggerated beyond effectiveness and intensified beyond artistry.

The Women at Point Sur (1927) portended that Jeffers' poetry would follow not *Roan Stallion* but *Tamar,* not unity but a thicket. That the thicket was brambly is revealed in a letter to James Rorty, which explains that *The Women at Point Sur* is supposed to assert the value of "old-fashioned morality"—as *Tamar* was supposed to, although *Tamar* "seemed to later thought to have a tendency to romanticize unmoral freedom." He adds:

Another intention, this time a primary one, was to show in action the danger of that Roan Stallion idea of "breaking out of humanity," misinterpreted in the mind of a fool or a lunatic. . . . just as Ibsen, in *The Wild Duck,* made a warning against his own idea in the hands of a fool, so *Point Sur* was meant to be a warning; but at the same time a reassertion.

He intended the rest of the book as:

1) An attempt to uncenter the human mind from itself. There is no health for the individual whose attention is taken up with his own mind and processes; equally there is no health for the society that is always introverted on its own members, as ours becomes more and more, the interest engaged inward in love and hatred, companionship and competition. These are

necessary, of course, but as they absorb all the interest they become fatal. All past cultures have died of introversion at last, and so will this one, but the individual can be free of the net, in his mind. It is a matter of "transvaluing values," to use the phrase of somebody that local people accuse me quite falsely of deriving from.

I have often used incest as a symbol to express these introversions, and used it too often.

2) The book was meant to be a tragedy, that is an exhibition of essential elements by the burning away through pain and ruin of inertia and the unessential.

3) A valid study in psychology; the study valid, the psychology morbid, sketching the growth of a whole system of emotional delusions from a "private impurity" that was quite hidden from consciousness until insanity brought it to the surface.

4) Therefore a partial and fragmentary study of the origin of religions; which have been necessary to society in the past, and I think remain necessary whether we like it or not, yet they derive from a "private impurity" of some kind in their originators.

5) A satire on human self-importance; referring back to (1).

6) A judgment of the tendencies of our civilization, which has very evidently turned the corner down hill.[15]

In view of these "intentions" it is not very astounding that *The Women at Point Sur* is even more tangled than *Tamar,* nor that the lines of the action are twisted into an almost hopeless snarl. Simplified as much as possible, the narrative assumes the following outline: "The Rev. Dr. Barclay" finds suddenly that he has nothing to say to his congregation and, deserting his pulpit as well as his wife and daughter, he wanders to Point Sur where he takes a room at the house of Natalia Morhead whose husband has not yet returned from the war. In Morhead's absence his father ("Old Morhead") has become a bedridden cripple, and Natalia has entered into a homosexual relationship with Faith Heriot, a waif who has suffered as a result of male brutality. Barclay ambles about the hills and in his incremental madness attracts disciples. To them he preaches Jeffers' Inhumanism adulterated with his own insanity and repressions. Meanwhile, his "private impurity" compels him to seek a sexual liaison with Maruca, an Indian woman. When his daughter, April, arrives with her mother to look after him, he contrives successfully to rape her. April bears the brunt not only of her father's difficulties but also of Rand Morhead's; for Randal returns at length from the war and falls vaguely in love with her. At the same time Faith Heriot becomes jealous of April because she thinks that Natalia's affections have been transferred to her. Eventually April, deranged by her rape and thinking that she is her brother Edward (killed in the war), determines to kill her father but kills herself instead. Barclay wanders on; his hypnotized disciples fall off one by one, and he dies of exhaustion alone in the wilderness.

Whatever rhetorical success the poem has, it fails to realize the manifold hopes that Jeffers entertained. Even as a study in abnormal psychology it is not successful, for the psychology with its excessive Freudian stratagems has merely the effect of mechanizing and defeating the characters. As for the poem's advocacy of "old-fashioned morality," it seems closer to what D. H. Lawrence would have called a "phallic" drama. Faith Heriot says toward the end, ". . . we are all turned up / Like needles to the . . . black maypole . . ." And the "black maypole":

. . . is what women
And drained old men want in their dreams,
What the empty bodies howl for.

This orgasm of death is the final impression of the poem,
and as such it seems more nearly a summons to a witches'
sabbath than an invitation to morality. The primary
trouble is, of course, as Jeffers admitted, the number of intentions. On the other hand it is these intentions which
make *The Women at Point Sur* important to a study of
Jeffers. It is the very matrix of his subsequent narratives.

As *Tamar* and *Roan Stallion* illustrate, Jeffers tended
in his earlier volumes to swing from pole to pole, and it is
not surprising that the volume to follow *The Women at
Point Sur—Cawdor* (1928)—admits of the least indebtedness to it. Nevertheless, *Cawdor* and *The Women at Point
Sur* are importantly bound to each other by the theme of
the return of the prodigal son. This theme, it will be remembered, stems from "The Vardens" in *Californians*.
Jeffers' prodigals do not return contritely, however, but as
destroyers. In *The Women at Point Sur* the theme is disguised as April Barclay's hallucination that she is her
brother and that she must kill her father. In *Cawdor* the
son does not consciously wish to destroy his father, but
destruction is the effective result of his return.

The notion of religion's originating in a "private impurity" was turned to account as the theme of Jeffers' next
volume, the drama *Dear Judas* (1929). Barclay's unconscious desire for incest is transfigured as Jesus' refusal
to believe that He is illegitimate. *Descent to the Dead*
(1931) is a short collection of reflective monodies deriving
from a sojourn in England and Ireland; it need not detain

us at this time, but *Thurso's Landing* (1932) returns both to the tortured repetitive strophes of *The Women at Point Sur* and to more than one of its themes. The lesbianism is repeated, and old Morhead's "chest-downward" incapacity is translated into an obvious castration motive—a motive which blends with that of the destroying prodigal, for in the attempt to destroy the memory of his dead father, Reave Thurso is maimed.

Give Your Heart to the Hawks (1933) continues the theme of the prodigal in the sense that Lance Fraser brutally tortures his father's mind. Another motive incorporated from the matrix is that of the messianic primitivism which Maruca, the Indian woman, personifies in *The Women at Point Sur*. As the frenzied people turn toward "the black maypole," Maruca flees to found a new world, believing that in her womb she carries:

> The Christ of the lions, for whom I shall kill fawns
> And feed him on the young of the mountains.

A similar fierce belief in the future characterizes Fayne, Lance's wife, in *Give Your Heart to the Hawks*. After murdering his brother, Lance cannot live up to Fayne's advice to trample, like Barclay, on the concepts of societal morality and he commits suicide. But, like Maruca, Fayne carries an unborn savior. She says that, though she could not save her husband, his unborn child "will change the world." *Solstice* (1935), based on the Medea legend, extends the portrait of the primitive mother. Like a jungle cat, Madrone Bothwell kills her children to prevent their being "touched" by another. In her extremity, of course, Madrone is a deliberate perversion of the messianic motive. *Solstice,* slight in itself and doubtless Jeffers' worst narrative, looks forward to the superb adaptation of Euripides' play in 1946.

The theme of incest reappears in 1937 with *Such Counsels You Gave to Me*. The narrative alludes to the well-known ballad, "Edward, Edward," but it also returns to *The Women at Point Sur*. "Edward" is Barclay's dead son and he enters not only the daughter's consciousness as her avenger but also into Barclay's.

> . . . a young man
> Approached him, what was it they were saying?
> Edward, Edward,
> Why does thy brand drip red with blood?

Howard Howren, then, in *Such Counsels You Gave to Me* is the Edward not only of the ballad but, in a psychic sense, also of *The Women at Point Sur*. He brings the motive of the destroying prodigal almost to a culmination. I say almost because the culmination must be reserved for *The Double Axe*.

Four years intervene between *Such Counsels You Gave to Me* and *Be Angry at the Sun* (1941) in which the narrative *Mara* is included. *Mara* considers the problem of conjugal infidelity, but the problem is explicated less in action than in Bruce Ferguson's arguments with his alter egos. These alter egos, which bear a resemblance to the theories of Jung, hark back to *The Women at Point Sur* where Barclay in his hysteria thinks he meets himself.

Two elements from the matrix enter *The Double Axe* (1948). First, *The Double Axe* harvests the related motives of the prodigal and of the Lazarus myth. Randal in *The Women at Point Sur* returns Lazarus-like from the war. In *Dear Judas* Lazarus appears not so much as the resurrected

man but as the man who refuses resurrection; he is the Inhumanist who is free of the net of human passions and he
argues against the painful ambitions of life. Hoult Gore in
The Double Axe partakes of both Lazarus and the prodigal.
A rotting corpse, he returns from his death on a Pacific
battlefield to destroy his father. The second element is Barclay's debate with himself. The one viable aspect of *The
Women at Point Sur* is Barclay's interior siege of himself,
his willful effort to attain to a condition of superior reality.
He says, "There is a power behind the appearances, you
will break through to it and touch it." But Barclay cannot,
for as he intensifies his struggle, the net more closely en-
meshes him and he succumbs to passion and illusion. By
contrast the old man in *The Double Axe* achieves an ideal
reality by cutting away his passions and illusions. He does
not besiege himself; he levels himself. Where *The Women
at Point Sur* satirized an improper application of Inhumanism, *The Double Axe* clarifies the proper application. Like
Nietzsche's Zarathustra, Barclay demands disciples and
power, declaring that there is no sin. The old man with his
singing double axe seeks solitude and only enough power
to control himself. The Inhumanist, he withdraws into an
inner salvation.

Because one cannot fail to suspect that the consistently
repeated theme of the destroying prodigal reveals the architecture of a personality, there is a temptation to make an
inductive leap at this point and to propose that the theme
suggests a father-reaction linked by the incest-theme to an
Oedipus complex. The temptation these days is, of course,
very great, but the proposition is not, I think, sound. In
poems written as late as 1941 which mention his father, a
gloomy tone of self-recrimination appears. To understand

this, one is helped by considering once again Jeffers' deliberate effacement of his emotive, bohemian period. In all likelihood Jeffers' guilt resulted not so much from what he felt to be his immoral deportment as from his feeling that he was outraging the standards of his father. It seems therefore probable that Jeffers' destroying prodigal implies not a "standard" Oedipus complex with a mother-fixation so readily as it implies that his narratives unconsciously attempt to revoke a source of moral guilt, for to remove the father would be to obliterate the code which he felt he had failed. In *Californians* (1916) Jeffers asked himself if he ought to call his father back from the grave, if he ought to "fee / That lost king's Endor-witch to answer me." When, however, some twenty years later in the poem "Come, Little Birds," he writes of consulting his father's ghost, Jeffers takes care that, though he confesses his sins, the ghost is unimpressed by them—or by his virtues: "He was patient and let me speak, but clearly not cared at all." Jeffers is absolved by the ghost's indifference, and importantly one finds no aggressive (Oedipal) overtone. This situation, as Jung in one of his case histories concludes, reflects neither hatred nor jealousy toward a father, but, on the contrary, emulation and reverence.

If Jeffers' narratives have assumed a dramatic form that seeks to blot out his father as one source of guilt based upon inferiority (in turn based upon idealization), his doctrine of Inhumanism emerges at a personal level as his effort to blot out the other source: himself. Ironically, we may turn his own concept of the origins of religion upon himself. Is not his desire to break out of humanity an extension of his desire to cast aside the adolescent period of incertitude and waste? That he has extended the repudiation of his own adolescence to mankind in general is underlined by his belief that modern man is immature: "It seems time that our race began to think as an adult does, rather than like an egocentric baby or insane person."[16]

Jeffers has wanted the world to rehearse his own phases of maturation. His attack on man is a continuation of his attack on himself, for the faults he attacks in his heroes are fickleness, sexual athleticism, and jealousy, and these are more nearly the faults of the adolescent hero than of the mature hero. They may be the problems of Romeo but they are not the problems of Macbeth. Because one repudiates the passions, however, does not mean that one is not fascinated by them; it may mean quite the opposite. And this seems to be the constant and nourishing tension in Jeffers' verse. As a philosopher he negates what as a human being he cannot do without.

II

Nietzsche and Schopenhauer

1

A MOST PERCEPTIVE—but also a somewhat misleading—comment on Robinson Jeffers was made by Joseph Warren Beach:

> He is perhaps the most realistic of all nature-poets. He is chief heir to that scientific tradition against which Tennyson and Browning struggled. He has never questioned the insignificance of man in the vast evolutionary scheme. And he finds no support for human dignity in an idealistic metaphysics which restores man's thought to the position of creator of reality.[1]

The statement is perceptive in that it recognizes Jeffers' siding with Darwin against the nineteenth-century idea of a "nature red in tooth and claw." But I must consider the statement misleading in that it tends to obscure the entirely indispensable touchstone to Jeffers' poetry: German Ideal philosophy.

Mr. Beach's conclusion is, of course, comprehensible, for the "scientific tradition" leads to exclusion of the tradition of an Ideal reality, and Mr. Beach is correct in holding that Jeffers does not allow man "the position of creator of reality." Nevertheless Jeffers attempts a grand, although awkward, synthesis of Idealism and pragmatism. The effort to compose these ideologies is documented in the poem "Love the Wild Swan."

> "I hate my verses, every line, every word.
> Oh pale and brittle pencils ever to try
> One grass-blade's curve, or the throat of one bird
> That clings to twig, ruffled against white sky.
> Oh cracked and twilight mirrors ever to catch
> One color, one glinting flash, of the splendor of things.
> Unlucky hunter, Oh bullets of wax,
> The lion beauty, the wild-swan wings, the storm of the
>   wings."
> —This wild swan of a world is no hunter's game.
> Better bullets than yours would miss the white breast,
> Better mirrors than yours would crack in the flame.
> Does it matter whether you hate your . . . self? At least
> Love your eyes that can see, your mind that can
> Hear the music, the thunder of the wings. Love the wild
>   swan.

Two quarreling conceptions direct the sonnet: the ordered program of Nature which relegates man to insignificance; and the subjective reality captured by the eye and the mind, which receive the impressions of order and beauty. But, quite as Mr. Beach advises us, if the eye and mind are capable of participation in divine reality they do not create it for Jeffers. Elsewhere we find the lines: "The beauty of things is not harnessed to human / Eyes and the little active minds: it is absolute."[2] Though this seems to contradict what I have just postulated, one must reconsider the word "absolute," whose connotations demand an infinite reality independent of empirical evidence. The eye and mind, then, although they are not responsible for the absolute, permit one to gain experience of it. And Jeffers' most recent position is indisputably clear: "The beauty of things —/ Is in the beholder's brain—the human mind's translation of their transhuman / Intrinsic value."[3] In part, of course, the mien of the experience is mystical, but the structure of the experience is founded on an idealistic metaphysics. This aspect of Jeffers' poetry has been strangely overlooked. I do not wish, however, to give the impression that criticism has ignored a German romanticism in Jeffers. The contrary is true. Yet the emphasis has centered in a Nietzschean influence, and that emphasis is not completely justified in a parallel reading of Jeffers and Nietzsche.

2

For a modern poet to admit to an "influence" is to invite wasps to build nests in his house. Nevertheless, Jeffers has made confessions of indebtedness to Nietzsche, and some critics have constructed unilateral hypotheses from his words, particularly from his statement in the "Foreword" to his *Selected Poetry:* "Another formative principle came to me from a phrase of Nietzsche's: 'The poets? The poets lie too much.'" To this may be added his earlier statement made in reference to *The Women at Point Sur* to the effect that the individual can in his own mind escape racial introversion by "'transvaluing values' to use the phrase of somebody that local people accuse me quite falsely of deriving from." The phrase "transvaluing values" recurs in *Thus Spake Zarathustra,* which Jeffers read as a youth in Switzerland, and Delmore Schwartz, H. H. Waggoner, Horace Gregory, and Amos Wilder have concluded that Nietzsche's philosophy is the most evident element in Jeffers' poetry. Eric Bentley goes so far as to place Jeffers in a fascist lineage of "Heroic Vitalists" who have followed Nietzsche in a "quest for a new immortality."[4] My own reading leads me to minimize the Nietzschean elements although not to discount them, for in the broadest terms Jeffers' poetry mirrors the intellectual power and austerity which we may sympathetically attribute to Nietzsche.

The greatness of Nietzsche is scarcely that of a technical philosopher but rather that of a forceful, poetic thinker whose influence on general culture has been profound. He tried to regard his contemporary world with the cold, fresh candor of the child who discovers and proclaims the absurdity of emperors. His attacks, hurled against what he considered mediocrity, decadence, and hypocrisy, disparaged everything that usually recommends itself to man: morals, religion, social progress. Against this negativism, however, he arrayed a positive belief in an ideal of Hellenic beauty and aristocratic vigor, attempting to establish on these foundations a new morality. In his Hegelian delight in paradox, he called himself the "first immoralist."

Nietzsche's deliberate exaggeration and paradox have concealed his more sentimental side and led to misunderstandings which culminated in the picture of him as an archetypal Nazi. Nietzsche was scarcely an anti-Semite nor did he envision a police state, but it is easy to pervert his wild statements into adumbrations of such things and to forget that "the good war which halloweth every cause" refers to the war of knowledge rather than to the battlefield. And even in the war of knowledge, though he professes to arm himself with godlessness and pitilessness, Zarathustra is sometimes a pathetic, a "lonesome" saint who may have nothing better to do than comfort a youth who reminds one of Werther or Manfred. Doubtless such a youth needs comforting, but it is not the stern superman, who has dissuaded himself utterly from pity, that one expects as the comforter.

These two aspects of the Nietzschean temperament—the imposing, hard surface and the disguised, interior mansuetude—derive from the effort to construct a positive belief from the materials of skepticism, and to erect a morality from the ruins of a theology overturned by pragmatism. Whatever failures and confusions attend it, the effort is courageous. And certainly Nietzsche's quest remains the primary quest for modern man. His effort and courage have necessarily affected vital minds. Even such disparate artists as André Gide and Robinson Jeffers have taken cognizance of Nietzsche's position. But we understand Jeffers' relation to Nietzsche best if we understand that many of their beliefs are incompatible. When Jeffers and Nietzsche touch, it is the accident of their both feeling for bearings in the same dark room.

Two of Jeffers' more idiosyncratic theories resemble Nietzsche's. First, as an obscurantist, Jeffers believes that no human epistemology can discover the entire nature of God. Naturally, then, he scorns formal theologies which essay to explain either God, or man's relationship to Him. In his poem "Theory of Truth" he supposes that Christ and Buddha developed their philosophies as a compensation for a personal deficiency. We may compare his notion with Nietzsche's similar, although not identical, belief that "every great philosophy up till now has consisted of . . . the confession of its originator, and a species of involuntary and unconscious autobiography."[5] Second, in his view of Christianity Jeffers speaks of the "tension" deriving from the incompatibility of "Western blood" and oriental Christianity.[6] And analyzing *At the Birth of an Age,* he says that "the Teutonic element began to warp and groan under the tension of Christian influence."[7] He is in this respect much like Nietzsche, who believed that the "Latin races" find Christianity more compatible with their temperament than do the northern "barbarous races" who have "poor talents for religion."[8] These are rather incidental concepts but they point toward Jeffers' significant symbolization of the tortured God, developed in several poems but most importantly in the drama *At the Birth of an Age.* The symbol is germane to Jeffers' religiosity and cryptic violence, but in Nietzsche's thought, while the concept appears clearly enough, it is not extended or foundational and perhaps it is negative.

In a more general way others have remarked that misanthropy, distrust of the city, and an aristocratic rejection of the crowd are common to Nietzsche and Jeffers. This, however, suggests nothing upon which to build theories. The attitudes are, after all, not bizarre.

3

The differences between Jeffers and Nietzsche are more significant than the likenesses. At the outset one cannot but be struck by the plea which Nietzsche makes for disciples; he cannot bear the solitude which he preaches. The very idea of disciples, however, is repulsive to Jeffers— if we accept his statements literally. In *The Double Axe,* when a youth desires to become the old man's follower, the conditions are not easy:

". . . My disciples must never sleep, except the nights when a full moon sets at midnight."

The young man said, "When is that?" And he considered and said: "You do not *want* disciples!"

"But how," the old man answered, "did you ever guess it?"

The old man may reflect something of Zarathustra's paradoxical negations, but one cannot stretch his mood to match Nietzsche's contempt for conventional morals and religion. Strict morality is for Jeffers the hallmark of a vigorous culture, and a similar conventionality informs his view of religion, in the sense of religion of faith rather than religion as ethic, for only religion stimulates societal morality. But, we may remember, Nietzsche with his perfect horror of any religion (excepting his personal one) repudiated Schopenhauer and Wagner for their "religious neurosis."

From their religious differences it is only a step to a very major disparity between Jeffers and Nietzsche: their separate reactions to mysticism. At first glance Zarathustra's rhapsodic and obscure utterances may suggest a mystical vision, and they do proceed toward it—only to reject it at the moment of ascension. Considering various concepts of God, Zarathustra says: "Evil do I call it and misanthropic: all that teaching about the one, and the plenum, and the unmoved, and the sufficient, and the imperishable!"[9] But Jeffers' God *is* the mystical "one, and the plenum, and the unmoved, and the sufficient, and the imperishable." His concept of God does not approximate the scholastic theory, but it is very near the Buddhistic conceptions. Again, however, to Nietzsche Buddha is not a mystic; he is a "profound physiologist."[10]

The problems of religion and mysticism bring up Jeffers' doctrine of Inhumanism, and it is in this connection

that one finds Jeffers irreconcilably opposed to the Nietzschean ideal. For Jeffers, to break away from humanity
means to turn from contemplation of self to contemplation
of God. But Nietzsche's idea of man's surpassing himself
means a turning from any contemplation of God to
an exclusive contemplation of man. I think that no two
philosophies could be more basically at odds than are Nietzsche's and Jeffers' at this crucial point. Curiously, however, certain details within their opposed beliefs wear a
deceptive appearance of similarity.

Nietzsche considered pain (as did Schopenhauer) the
illuminator and informant of life. "Happiness," therefore,
occupies a precarious place. When Zarathustra presents
himself as "the wickedest of all fishers of men," the bait he
uses is—oddly enough—"happiness." Does happiness, then,
for Nietzsche merely conceal the pain of the hook? Or, is
happiness insignificant except as a decoy? The answer to
both questions is probably "yes," but I am content to leave
the implications of Zarathustra's statement in question
form.

Jeffers' idea of happiness has undergone change. In
1938 he wrote:

Human happiness? If a harmless drug were invented under the influence of which all people could be intensely and
harmoniously happy, only working enough to provide each
other with sustenance and the drug—would that be a good goal
for men? That would be maximum happiness, minimum pain.
. . . I am not answering the question—at present.[11]

When Jeffers comes finally to answer the question, as he
does in recent (1951) verse, he modifies his Nietzschean

mockery, writing simply: "I have learned that happiness is important."

The attitude toward happiness which is an indulgence of self is connected with the attitude toward pity which is an indulgence of others. Nietzsche's war with Christianity quite instinctively took the form of negating the Christian values, among which is pity. Although Nietzsche is sometimes ambivalent here, Zarathustra mocks "at all pity," and in *Ecce Homo* Nietzsche wrote that "it is only among decadents that this *pity* is called a virtue."[12] Jeffers, it is true, often seems pitiless. Yet, once again, his latest position is an amendment. In the poem "The World's Wonders," published first in 1951, he sums up his life's experience and adds:

> It is easy to know the beauty of inhuman things, sea, storm and mountain; it is their soul and their meaning.
> Humanity has its lesser beauty, impure and painful; we have to harden our hearts to bear it.
>
> I have hardened my heart only a little: I have learned that happiness is important, but pain *gives* importance.
> The use of tragedy: Lear becomes as tall as the storm he crawls in; and a tortured Jew became God.

This seems not a voice that mocks compassion but a dirge for man's failure to come to terms with himself. The failure to Jeffers is so monstrous that it is bearable only when he has secured a sense of detachment wherein he renders the spectacle of man's struggles tolerable by envisioning them as a manifestation of divine will. Thus, although doomed, man assumes a supramundane grandeur. But to be involved, to leave one's seat and to storm onto the stage—that way madness lies. This spectator of doom with the slightly hardened heart is far from Nietzsche, the self-conscious hero, gathering disciples to implement a triumphant finale.

To be a spectator of life—purely a spectator—is, however, to deny life in its richest sense. In this way most basically Jeffers is the antipodes of Nietzsche, who asserted life above every other value. Now, one may perceive that this difference between Jeffers and Nietzsche is also a prime difference between Nietzsche and Schopenhauer. Schopenhauer had proclaimed the nullification of the wish to live as the supreme wisdom. Nietzsche had respected Schopenhauer—had respected him mainly as the opponent of a mediocre optimism stemming from Hegel—but Nietzsche rejected Schopenhauer, for his own aspiration was the emphasis—above all things—of life. And in one other essential Nietzsche rejected Schopenhauer—again in a direction oppositional to the attitudes of Jeffers. I refer to the matter of "immoralism," for Schopenhauer distinctly preached the need for a common moral code.

Nietzsche may have consciously recorded his rejection of Schopenhauer in "Zarathustra's Prologue." As Zarathustra begins his "down-going" into the world of humanity, an old man asks him what he proposes to do "in the land of the sleepers," why go there at all? Zarathustra gives as his reason his love of mankind. The old man counters that he has been driven to solitude because he once "loved men too well," but that now he loves God, not men. The attitudes of this old hermit could be those of Schopenhauer, and this seems significant since these are the attitudes that Zarathustra must repudiate at the very outset of his career. It is to Schopenhauer that Jeffers bears a resemblance, and not, as critics for the past twenty years have been insisting, to Nietzsche.

Yet, once again, the problem is not one of direct influence, but a problem of the direction the human temperament and intellect can be expected to take when confronted by a given set of compulsions and alternatives. The essential concern in Schopenhauer, the relation of matter and idea, is an essential concern in Jeffers. And Schopenhauer's conclusion in this respect is identical with Jeffers' insistence that there exists a superior reality behind appearance, a reality which is discoverable, though not easily so. It would seem in the final analysis that Jeffers and Nietzsche represent two opposed responses to the Schopenhauerian concept. Nietzsche selected and altered Schopenhauer's configuration of the Will, while he rejected the mystical conception of Idea. But Jeffers exemplifies the temperament that chooses to emphasize a mysticism in order to find a universal unity.

4

The problem of human suffering has been paramount in Jeffers' poetic development. He supposes that the ultimate purpose of pain is discovery. This intuition approximates Nietzsche's feeling, but Nietzsche is in this respect indebted to Schopenhauer. For Schopenhauer pain was inevitable, since to remove positive pain is to beget ennui, which is a form of pain. "Great suffering," however, is desirable because it releases one from sensitivity to "lesser ills" while "freedom from great suffering makes even the most trifling inconveniences torment us and put us out of humour."[13] For Jeffers, too, the substitution of a great suffering for a lesser ill permits discovery of God. Accordingly, he advises that one should not expect the triumph of "justice or happiness" either in personal life or in the social whole. "These dreams," he tells us, "will not be fulfilled."[14]

For both Jeffers and Schopenhauer the desirability of substituting the greater for the lesser suffering is postulated on two conditions: first, that life is an illusion—for Jeffers the "net," for Schopenhauer the "web of Maya"—and, second, that social effort is empty. Schopenhauer wrote that "we are forced to concede to the poets that life is a long dream."[15] And for Jeffers the cosmic purpose of consciousness is merely this—the dreaming, sometimes the nightmare of Nature. But there is a compensation. Following Plato, Schopenhauer said that "the philosopher strives to awake himself," and Jeffers believes that one can awake, however rarely, to see "through the trick to the beauty."

Because the activities of man are those of dreamy unreality, there is, in Schopenhauer's mind, no good reason to enter into common pursuits, and indeed man in the herd is ignoble. The good man will therefore love solitude, and ". . . on passing his fortieth year, any man of the slightest power of mind—any man, that is who has more than the sorry share of intellect with which Nature has endowed five-sixths of mankind—will hardly fail to show some trace of misanthropy."[16]

The two attitudes which elicit Schopenhauer's "misanthropy" are "either/or" attitudes. Life is either trivial pain *or* great suffering; life is either illusion *or* the attempt to awake. The nature of this thinking implies both what the superior man will do and that this superior man (the philosopher) is rare. Once superiority and rarity have been posited, then the "virtues" of misanthropy and solitude should follow. And once misanthropy and solitude can be established as virtues, then an unconventional code develops—in Schopenhauer, sanctification of death; in Jeffers, the doctrine of Inhumanism. In all of this there abides no support for traditional humanism. The individual is sacrificed; the species alone remains important and Nature alone is immortal, for in her manifold forms Nature is the material expression of pure Idea. Man's comfort derives from contemplating the continuity and renewal of Nature. Yet the consolation of immortality in Nature is not the highest attainment possible to man. Schopenhauer considers it possible (at moments) to bypass the will to live and to enter directly and immediately into the Idea:

... the comprehension of genius, is conditioned by a silence of the will so profound that while it lasts even the individuality vanishes from consciousness and the man remains *as the pure subject of knowing,* which is the correlative of the *Idea.*[17]

Consolation in Nature and identification with Idea (or God) also enter into Jeffers' central thought. Surveying the "noble hill-tops," the old man in *The Double Axe,* kneeling, weeping, addresses the universe:

> Dear love. You are so beautiful.
> Even this side the stars and below the moon. How can you
> be ... all this ... and me also?
> Be human also? The yellow puma, the flighty mourning-
> dove and flecked hawk, yes, and the rattlesnake
> Are in the nature of things; they are noble and beautiful
> As the rocks and the grass—not this grim ape,
> Although it loves you.—Yet two or three times in my life
> my walls have fallen—beyond love—no room for love—
> I have been you.

Schopenhauer's complex of ideas dictates his concept of tragedy (a concept which no German romantic philosopher seems able to do without): suffering is a purifier which permits man to silence his will to live so that he enters into "the complete knowledge of the nature of the world. . . . Thus we see in tragedies the noblest men, after long conflict and suffering, at last renounce the ends they have so keenly followed, and all the pleasures of life for ever, or else freely and joyfully surrender life itself."[18] Jeffers' Orestes in *The Tower Beyond Tragedy* almost too perfectly realizes Schopenhauer's concept. Through his suffering he is able to "fall in love outward," rejecting ambition and passion and flowing into the pure beauty of an ideal reality where there is "no color but clearness" and "no passion but peace" and "no time but spheral eternity." Orestes in effect excises the Dionysian element which Nietzsche insisted on in his definition of tragedy.

5

It seems desirable to re-emphasize that while Jeffers is contiguous in certain respects with Nietzsche, his basic position is remote from Nietzsche's in the degree that it is close to Schopenhauer's. This is the main point which I wish to make. But how seriously may one accept the parallels with Nietzsche or with Schopenhauer? The reasonable answer lies, I think, in recognizing that these nineteenth-century Germanic elements help us to determine the limits of Jeffers' verse. They are important to the whole of contemporary culture and they are specifically important to Jeffers—but not so much in themselves as in the way he has combined them with other elements. The tortured God of Nietzsche and the Schopenhauerian concept of "life as pain" combine with Jeffers' instinctive religious intensity. The pessimism of Schopenhauer and the stormy, paradoxical skepticism of Nietzsche inspired Oswald Spengler and reinforce Jeffers' own Spenglerian views. Nietzsche, in his own right and in his effect on modern psychology, is an important ingredient in the modern atavistic faith. In proper context it will be possible to demonstrate that Jeffers' view of science tends to reassert Schopenhauer's compromised Idealism. Most importantly, however, it can be observed that while all of these considerations—religiosity, Spenglerism, atavism, and science—interact to produce Jeffers' credo, the spirit of that credo can be traced if not to Schopenhauer at least to the problems that Schopenhauer courageously faced up to. For if one's universe is fractured by intense antagonisms between matter and idea, one may, like Schopenhauer and Jeffers, pay homage to such seemingly separate, irreconcilable thinkers as Buddha and Lucretius. But in the mind which yearns to compose its universe, Buddha and Lucretius are reconciled by their similar aims of serenity.

III

The Broken Balance

1

WHEN BRUCE FERGUSON, the hero of *Mara* (1941), finds himself unable to understand why his life has lost all centrality and why wasteful passions lead him and his wife to dreary entanglements, he retreats to half-forgotten college books and reads Oswald Spengler's *The Decline of the West*. The mystical theory of ineluctable culture-cycles represents "truth," an explanation for his difficulties. But this truth is "poisonous," and he takes his own life. Bruce Ferguson, Jeffers tells us in a different poem ("For Una"), is in "some ways / My very self but mostly my antipodes." Presumably he is unlike Jeffers in yielding to suicide. But in his Augustinian suspicions and in his relating his psychological plight to a Spenglerian hypothesis, he embodies two important themes of Jeffers' poetry.

In 1941 Jeffers told a Harvard audience:

> The idea of culture-ages—culture-cycles—the patterned rise and decline of one civilization after another—is a commonplace now, nearly as commonplace as death or war, but it held my

thought and has been a frequent subject of my verses—"The Fall of an Age," "The Birth of an Age," and so forth. The idea was popularized by Oswald Spengler's book, "Decline of the West"; but it came to me much earlier, from my own thoughts, and then I found it formulated by the English Egyptologist, Flinders Petrie, in a little volume called "The Revolutions of Civilization," first published in 1911. Of course it was developed long before that, notably by Vico of Naples, Giovanni Battista Vico, who published his book in 1725. And there is a passage in Plutarch's "Life of Sulla," referring to the Etruscan acceptance of this idea, which I versified in one of several pieces called "The Broken Balance."

Although it is clear from the youthful poetry that Petrie and Spengler did not create Jeffers' endemic fatalism, I think it likely that they confirmed him in a set of dualisms intellectually related to that fatalism: a dualism between Nature and history, a dualism between Nature and man, a dualism between culture and civilization. The first of these is the premise for the others and may be expressed in Spengler's terms: "*Nature* and *History* are the opposite extreme terms of man's range of possibilities, whereby he is enabled to order the actualities about him as a picture of the world."[1]

There is nothing startling in the concept, but in a special type of mind—intense, continuously focused on this matter—endorsement of such a premise compels acceptance of the corollary that "Man-knowing and Nature-knowing are in essence entirely incapable of being compared . . ."[2] For man and Nature are different just as animal life is different from vegetable life:

Servitude and freedom—this is in last and deepest analysis the differentia by which we distinguish vegetable and animal existence. Yet only the plant is wholly and entirely what it is; in the being of the animal there is something dual. A vegetable is only a vegetable; an animal is a vegetable and something more besides. A herd that huddles together trembling in the presence of danger, a child that clings weeping to its mother, a man desperately striving to force a way into his God—all these are seeking to return out of the life of freedom into the vegetal servitude from which they were emancipated into individuality and loneliness.[3]

The difference, then, between man and Nature, animal and vegetable, is consciousness, wherein repose the properties of volition, choice, and individuality. The idea is sufficiently obvious that most minds are indifferent to it. But to some it is of the essence. We may instance the traditional theology wherein "self-consciousness" is the origin of sin. In the Spenglerian and Jeffersian universe, consciousness becomes a source of distress that drives man and his civilizations to seek death.

The separation of man and Nature is basic, but the correlative separation of "culture" and "civilization"—the "becoming" and the "become"—is of greater pertinence to our study. Spengler thought of the active, growing historical organism as "becoming," and he called this flourishing, explorative state, "culture." "Civilization" he thought of as the attainment of complete growth beyond which nothing except decline is possible:

A culture is born in the moment when a great soul awakens out of the proto-spirituality (*dem urseelenhaften Zustande*) of ever-childish humanity, and detaches itself, a form from the formless, a bounded and mortal thing from the boundless and enduring. It blooms on the soil of an exactly-definable landscape, to which plant-wise it remains bound. It dies when this

soul has actualized the full sum of its possibilities in the shape
of peoples, languages, dogmas, arts, states, sciences, and reverts
into the proto-soul. But its living existence, that sequence of
great epochs which define and display the stages of fulfilment,
is an inner passionate struggle to maintain the Idea against the
powers of Chaos without and the unconscious muttering deep-
down within. . . . The aim once attained—the idea, the entire
content of inner possibilities, fulfilled and made eternally actual
—the Culture congeals, its force breaks down, and it becomes
Civilization, the thing which we feel and understand in the
words Egypticism, Byzantinism, Mandarinism. . . .

This—the inward and outward fulfilment, the finality, that
awaits every living Culture—is the purport of all the historic
"declines," amongst them that decline of the Classical which we
know so well and fully, and another decline, entirely comparable to it in course and duration, which will occupy the first
centuries of the coming millennium but is heralded already and
sensible in and around us to-day—the decline of the West.[4]

These paragraphs contain Spengler's essential motivation:
the necessity of growth and decline, the permanence of
Nature and the deduction that decline has begun to set in
over the Western world. On this last score he is willing
to be most definite, writing that "the inward *finishedness
(Fertigsein)* . . . will set in from about the year 2000."[5]

Jeffers' poetry has contemplated a society which he
feels is about to enter its period of "finishedness." Like
Spengler, he sees the present as the last evolution of the
period of "Culture," the sunset glow of the final greatness
of the age. From "The Broken Balance":

> The world sickens with change, rain becomes poison,
> The earth is a pit, it is time to perish.
> The vines are fey, the very kindness of nature
> Corrupts what her cruelty before strengthened.

When you stand on the peak of time it is time to begin to
     perish.

But the final collapse he tells us in "I Shall Laugh Purely"
is centuries away. "It is not so late as you think: give nature
time." Meanwhile he sees Western man in love with luxury
and machines, inclining toward subjective passions—love,
hate, jealousy—and dissipating his energies in minute, if
painful, quarrels. The subjectivity mirrors the subjectivity
of the declining civilization. "All the world is slipping to
cinders about us and love is all that there is," howls David
Carrow in that early ambitious and quaint poem *The
Coast-Range Christ*. But even this passionate introspection
surrenders to a further manifestation of exhaustion, the
condition that Spengler termed "second religiousness," the
penultimate expression of a culture-cycle, when the "soul
thinks once again, and in Romanticism looks back piteously
to its childhood . . ."[6] We may discover the idea dramatized
at the end of *The Women at Point Sur,* but Jeffers has also
given it the attention of a short poem "Thebaid."

How many turn back toward dreams and magic, how many
     children
Run home to Mother Church, Father State,
To find in their arms the delicious warmth and folding of
     souls.
The age weakens and settles home toward old ways.
An age of renascent faith: Christ said, Marx wrote, Hitler
     says,
And though it seems absurd we believe.
Sad children, yes. It is lonely to be adult, you need a father.
With a little practise you'll believe anything.

A "renascent faith," according to Spengler, is ancillary
to the "death wish" in the eroded civilization: "The last

man of the world-city no longer *wants* to live—he may
cling to life as an individual, but as a type, as an aggregate,
no, for it is a characteristic of this collective existence that
it eliminates the terror of death."[7] The voice of this exhaustion mutters bleakly through many of the narratives. In
Such Counsels You Gave to Me, after the mother and
son have poisoned the father, Jeffers comments:

> They had still a fair chance of intact life, they pre-
> ferred despair.
> They were in fact exhausted, and the waters of their minds
> draining away
> Left high and clear the common desire of death, that stands
> like a drowned tower in all human minds,
> The waters of life cover it and hide it: now it stood dark and
> tall from the water, a forgotten tower
> In a drained lake: the astonished discoverers
> Wade out through mud and water to enter the door, under
> the lake-weed lintel-fringes, and climb
> The ooze-choked stair.

Here there is some difficulty in establishing whether we
are confronted by a personal fascination with death or with
an objective dramatization of an idea, but probably we are
confronted by both. In any case, the idea of a societal death
wish appears to be dramatized in *Thurso's Landing.*

Thurso's Landing opens with "the coast road . . .
being straightened and repaired again," an imputation of
megalopolitan encroachment. The poem progresses to a
hunting scene, contrasting the simple country man, Reave
Thurso, against his wife Helen, who is both fascinated and
repelled by the blood and death of the hunt. We are to see
her as attracted to the primitive vigor of brutality even

though at the same time she expresses a decadence characterized by purely personal, trivial values.

Behind this crucial contrast and Helen's ambivalence billows the cloud of the first World War, from which Mark, Reave's brother, has returned lame. And like the war, intrusive but vague, hovers the ghost-presence of the dead father who, having failed in life, has committed suicide (prior to the opening of the poem). But his failure ironically lives on in a useless steel cable suspended across a chasm, the vestige of the father's unsuccessful attempt to quarry limestone. Helen Thurso elopes into the desert with a lover, Rick Armstrong; Reave pursues and brings her back to the Landing. On her return she encounters the complication of Reave's temporary mistress, the sad, weak Hester. Adding to this difficulty, Mark, her brother-in-law, falls in love with her; his passion, along with the effect of his war experience and the haunting presence of the father's failure, drives Mark mad. In a symbolic effort to set things right, to remove the atmosphere of decay and defeat, Reave decides to cut down the steel cable. But as the strands of the cable sever, it lashes erratically, breaking his back. Mark hangs himself. At the end Helen cuts Reave's throat, releasing him from torture and sterility, then poisons herself.

Removed from the texture of the poem, the synopsis is lugubrious. But the characters create a poetic, if not real, life by confirming the theme of the death wish at different levels of intensity. Because he has been most deeply affected by society, Mark longs for death most explicitly, mirroring the death wish of civilization, and listening to what Jeffers significantly calls "the false prophet." Helen vacillates between a fear of death and a love of death. Reave, remaining most nearly emblematic of the peasant-strengths, fights stubbornly against dying, even after he has been maimed. As Helen cuts his throat, he forms "his lips to say 'Bitch,' / But breath and the light" fail. And it is worth emphasizing that Jeffers' admiration clearly goes to Reave, for the widespread notion that to Jeffers the death wish is a desirable or intelligent emotion is false. The idea is infused with great psychic turbulence as well as dignity, as death always has been, and it is not to Jeffers an evil desire. But "endurance," he says, is "death's nobler cousin."[8]

2

The acceptance of a Spenglerian doom is obviously commensurate with the polarity of death and resurrection in the structure of Jeffers' temperament. But to this *primum mobile* we must add Jeffers' Schopenhauerian tendency to regard the species rather than the individual and to relate all human matters to a historical basis. To this tendency he has sacrificed certain elements of psychological realism in his narratives. Curiously enough, the reason for this sacrifice may be fixed by Spengler's words:

The world of incident is the world of once-actual facts that longingly or anxiously we live forward to (entgegenleben) as Future, that raise or depress us as the living Present, and that we contemplate with joy or with grief as Past. The world of causes and effects is the world of the constantly-possible, of the timeless truths which we know by dissection and distinction. . . .

Only the insight that can penetrate into the metaphysical is capable of experiencing in data *symbols* of that which happened, and so of elevating an incident into a Destiny. . . .

It is this insight that constitutes the singularity and the power of Shakespeare . . . he is *the Dramatist of the Incidental.* And yet this Incidental is the very heart of Western tragedy, which is a true copy of the Western history idea and with it gives the clue to that which we understand in the world [*sic*] —so misconstrued by Kant—"Time." It is incidental that the political situation of "Hamlet," the murder of the King and the succession question impinge upon just that character that Hamlet is.[9]

This passage suggests that Shakespeare's characters reveal (metaphysically) that they belong inextricably to a destiny which looks back and forward while it is contained in the present, and there is some interest in comparing Spengler's concept with Jeffers' poem "Haunted Country":

> Here the human past is dim and feeble and alien to us
> Our ghosts draw from the crowded future.
> Fixed as the past how could it fail to drop weird shadows
> And make strange murmurs about twilight?
> In the dawn twilight metal falcons flew over the mountain,
> Multitudes, and faded in the air; at moonrise
> The farmer's girl by the still river is afraid of phantoms,
> Hearing the pulse of a great city
> Move on the water-meadow and stream off south; the country's
> Children for all their innocent minds
> Hide dry and bitter lights in the eye, they dream without knowing it
> The inhuman years to be accomplished,
> The inhuman powers, the servile cunning under pressure,
> In a land grown old, heavy and crowded.
> There are happy places that fate skips; here is not one of them;
> The tides of the brute womb, the excess
> And weight of life spilled out like water, the last migration
> Gathering against this holier valley-mouth

That knows its fate beforehand, the flow of the womb,
    banked back
By the older flood of the ocean, to swallow it.

One could account for any similitude between Spengler's
"world of incident" and Jeffers' "valley-mouth that knows
its fate beforehand" on the grounds that such would be a
likely coincidence in minds highly historical in their enthusiasms, but the explanation is not deeply important. The
poem is essential to an understanding of the narrative
poems, for it establishes that Jeffers is not claimed by the
ordinary time-dimension of art. His narratives lean back
upon the past and stretch forward into a future—a future
complicated, neurotic. This intent explains what must
otherwise seem a contradiction too absurd to merit serious
investigation: the contradiction between "primitive" characters and their decadent behavior. To understand the
characters at all, one must understand that they reflect past,
present, and future historicity. They represent Western
man in three aspects. One may logically observe, of course,
that characters who belong to no absolute time cannot be
"real." Often they are not. Sometimes they seem only Jeffers' phantoms created to save himself from the "wolves"
of "pain and terror, the insanities of desire" over which he
broods in "Apology for Bad Dreams":

> I imagined victims for those wolves, I made them
>   phantoms to follow,
> They have hunted the phantoms and missed the house.

3

It is easy to find fault with Spengler's history, to point
to the dogmatism, the weakness of arguing from analogy,

the oracular mysticism. These faults may in poetry be virtues. The tyranny of culture cycles, attended by suffering and human confusion, permits Jeffers to re-create a condition of fate similar to the classical concept. The contemplation of an inescapable decline may be an esthetic experience both terrifying and—in the vastness of the stage—magnificent. But Jeffers takes no sadistic pleasure in the suffering of the individual:

> I would burn my right hand in a slow fire
> To change the future . . . I should do so foolishly. The beauty of modern
> Man is not in the persons but in the
> Disastrous rhythm, the heavy and mobile masses, the dance of the
> Dream-led masses down the dark mountain.

So Jeffers wrote in "Rearmament" (1932). In 1948 his belief is unchanged, but he is more explicit. "How beautiful," he writes in *The Double Axe,* "are these risings / And fallings: the waves of the sea, the Athenian empire, / The civilization of Europe, the might of America." But why, one asks, why "beautiful"? Jeffers answers:

> God and the tragic poets
> They love this pattern; it is like the beauty of a woman to them;
> They cannot refrain from it. What goes high they bring down.

The Spenglerian landscape is an esthetic, tragic, religious landscape. Neither dwarfing nor inflating man, it silhouettes him against the somber colors of the late sunset, which, Jeffers always reminds us, must fade to darkness. Always aware of the fading, Jeffers' poetry extends the traditional frame of tragedy, beyond the individual, the household, the nation. Disintegration obtains to the species, to the planets, to solar systems and galaxies. Like Spengler, he imagines the death of "man himself, and beyond man the phenomenon of plant and animal existence on the earth's surface, the earth, the sun, the whole world of sun-systems."[10] But, however complete the vista of dissolution may be, we observe that it is also postponed. Unlike Chaucer's carpenter in *The Miller's Tale*, Jeffers has no anticipation of immediate catastrophe. His vision permits the luxury of the sad prospect without imposing immediate danger. Yet the vision is not entirely bare of immediacy. The contemplation of ruin springs not merely from a love of final things but partly from a detestation of present circumstances, an impatience with things as they are, a feeling that until the nadir has been reached no ascent is possible. Destruction returns man to paradise. Thus, in common with most apocalyptic longings, the surge toward annihilation is coupled with a faith in a messianic restitution. For Jeffers the phoenix is Siva, the Hindu god-goddess of destruction and renewal, who, when she has destroyed even "the wild white swan of the beauty of things,"

> Then she will be alone, pure destruction, achieved and su-
> preme,
> Empty darkness under the death-tent wings.
> She will build a nest of the swan's bones and hatch a new
> brood,
> Hang new heavens with new birds, all be renewed.

The eschatological vision is as old as man but it is one which has been treated with the greatest intensity in the twentieth century. Spengler as a philosopher and Jeffers as a poet have given it the strongest attention, but they are neither alone nor the first. Indeed, it is difficult to summon up many contemporary writers who in one way or another have not emphasized a climate of decline. But we may confine our attention to the poet who, Jeffers has said, is the great poet of our period, William Butler Yeats, and to the poet whom Jeffers has recognized as the most "influential," T. S. Eliot.[11]

Yeats, like many another after the first World War, read Spengler, and, while he cannot be said to have derived ideas from *The Decline of the West,* it is likely that he felt it confirmed his own thinking. One needs only to adduce his poem "The Second Coming" for an exact example of the eschatological vision linked to the messianic vision; a moving and grim example. As for Eliot, it is perhaps too well known to need additional commentary that he was haunted by the idea of society in a condition of spiritual dryness. In somnambulating through the waste land Eliot was not interested precisely in the condition of decline as an aspect in a large historical drama, although his paraphrase of "great" lines in less than great contexts possesses an irony which is at heart historical. But, like Yeats, he linked the waste land to a vision of rejuvenation.

Yeats, Eliot, and Jeffers offer different responses to the malaise of modern man. If in politics Yeats inclined toward a principle of control such as offered hope also to D. H. Lawrence and Ezra Pound, in his personal philosophy he moved toward an ideal of inorganic passivity, toward becoming the golden bird of an emperor. For that matter Yeats always tended toward a passiveness. (His early love poems were sometimes written from the viewpoint of the woman, as is his treatment of the Leda myth later on.)

And Yeats' inorganic repose is not totally unlike Jeffers' mystical ideal of being absorbed into the atoms of the divine universe. But does not mysticism naturally recommend itself to the modern, "explained" world? Eliot, too, as *The Waste Land* adumbrated, has inclined toward a mysticism as a release from spiritual discomfort.

For Yeats and Eliot the solution, the antidote, seems to me a retreat: for the one a mysticism of superstition; for the other a mysticism of the past, a slow ritualistic dance among the symbols of medieval Catholicism. Jeffers, I suppose, has no "solution." But he takes a position which would in his view preserve the individual mind and soul: his doctrine of Inhumanism. This cool belief assumes a Spenglerian objectivity toward the maze of history, an ability to view "the whole fact of Man from an immense distance, to regard the individual Cultures, one's own included, as one regards the range of mountain peaks along a horizon."[12] In his poetry the doctrine is advanced as a way of maintaining sanity in a madhouse.

IV

The Brain Vault

1

THE STRAINED RELATIONSHIP between matter and idea which burdened Schopenhauer in the early nineteenth century hardly troubled the positivists, for they could deny the strain by denying any relationship. Comte admired the medieval separation of secular from sacramental concerns and he demonstrated his admiration by abandoning the search for ultimate causes. To the positivistic way of thinking, the phenomenon itself was the ultimate significance, and, operating from this precept, Herbert Spencer attempted to relate psychology, sociology, and ethics to the phenomenon of organic growth. Natural laws were as sacred to him as "revealed religion" was to the divine.

The concept of natural law as the basis for historical theory, for esthetics and ethics, produced the "scientific" philosopher, such as Spencer in the nineteenth century and Havelock Ellis in the twentieth. In a measure, too, this concept stands behind the poetry of Thomas Hardy and Robinson Jeffers. Yet it is quite wrong to suppose that Jeffers is very like Spencer; it is not wrong to suppose that he is somewhat like Havelock Ellis. The degree of similarity is contained in the extent to which Ellis represents the transition between nineteenth-century positivism and the metaphysical floundering—a transition between positivism and the humbled, less arrogant science—of the twentieth century.

Ellis felt compelled to wander away from natural laws without ever feeling compelled to abandon them completely. At heart he wanted an ethics consonant with both a vigorous naturalism and a satisfying idealism. But no matter to what altitudes his soul yearned, his emphasis on natural laws induced him to admire life primarily as a vital force and to see it, as does Jeffers, in relation to its primitive origins.

Jeffers evidently respected Ellis, for he sent him a copy of *Roan Stallion, Tamar and Other Poems,* and Ellis wrote a brief, although warm appreciation of it.[1] In his immersion in life, his faith in it, Havelock Ellis would seem almost certainly the opposite of Jeffers; but actually in other ways they have much in common. Without any intention of practising, both studied medicine in order to know as much as possible about the basic nature of life. It was as if they were paying whatever debts are due matter so as to move with impunity toward metaphysics. Science, as such, contented neither of them, but they did not feel that they could transcend it by remaining ignorant of it. And the transcending was important. Ellis' whole attitude continuously rehearses a movement from phenomena to philosophy. It is not accident that his *Psychology of Sex* begins with "The Biology of Sex" and terminates with "Sublimation," for always the idea of progressing from the basic reality to the highest form of experience brought him his greatest satisfaction, the feeling that "life is art," proclaimed in *The Dance of Life*. He was willing to believe with Plato "that love was a plant of heavenly growth." But he wanted to be certain that the premises for the belief were intact, certain, and anchored, that the plant had "its roots in the earth."[2] Jeffers' method, too, is that of beginning with the undeniable fact of matter and thence progressing toward what is not matter of fact: not toward life as art but toward life as an aspect of God.

To concentrate one's attention on the laws of Nature is to become aware that man's behavior is often inharmonious with the appearance of order in the universe. This discrepancy stimulated the famous scorn of Democritus, but it may lead easily beyond mockery to the bitter awareness of the lonely and wayward separation of man from his universe. The viewpoint may manifest itself in a satirical withdrawal in which the knowledge of Nature is employed with deadly sarcasm. From Havelock Ellis:

The way you make the creature if you are God—or whatever one may choose to call It—is as follows: After well mixing, stirring, and chopping up, you form a tube of two layers of cells and allow them to adhere to each other to form a third. So you have a sack for absorbing food from the circumambient water or air—being careful to leave one or two little holes—and for thereby growing; all the rest follows in time; the outer layer puts forth a sensory and motor nervous system to aid in the nourishing process, and the whole sack puts forth four limbs which gradually elongate and enable the sack to push itself towards the most attractive food streams. Then you place it on its two hind-limbs so that it may swing from one on to the other and so be able to move more rapidly towards its food, as well as to seek after or run away from its fellow-creatures, and generally to debase the face of the earth and destroy all other living things, animal or vegetable, while its two fore-limbs may be used to grab its food and to embrace or to kill its fellows . . .[3]

In his different idiom Jeffers writes that "the breed of man / Has been queer from the start. It looks like a botched experiment that has run wild and ought to be stopped."[4]

Satirical repudiation of the "botched experiment" is only one of possible manifestations of the viewpoint which separates man and Nature. The naturalist may choose to focus attention momentarily or even exclusively upon man in order to satisfy himself as to why man is an alien perversity in Nature. When the naturalist takes this step he quite obviously is confronted with the multiple problems of the human mind. For some, like Havelock Ellis, psychology constituted a step in the stairway leading from a materialist base toward a new spiritual meaning.

2

Although Jeffers has made obvious use of the theories of modern psychology, his attitude has been one of caution:

I read several works of and about Freud and Jung, and found the first one rather ridiculous, but changed my mind. That was probably in 1914 or so. I still think that Freud pioneered a new sort of knowledge, however limited or fanciful its later developments. The use of incest as a symbol is no doubt connected with those dream-studies.[5]

Whatever his qualifications, Jeffers deliberately set out to dramatize the new psychology in *The Women at Point Sur*. It will be remembered that he confessed to James Rorty that he wanted "the study valid, the psychology morbid, sketching the growth of a whole system of emotional delusions from a 'private impurity' " that remained "hidden from consciousness until insanity brought it to the surface." And this emphasis upon "morbid" psychology suggests what a reading of the poetry will demonstrate: an early preoccupation with Freudian theory.

As is perhaps too well known, Sigmund Freud's great contribution to modern knowledge is the theory of the "unconscious." The theory assumes that the unconscious surfaces in dream symbolism as a "wish-fulfilment," subtending, at the lowest stratum, to the earliest phases of childhood. In neurotic states the "wish-impulses" are disguised sexual impulses from infancy which have been repressed during maturation. Like many of his contemporaries, Jeffers has used sexual symbolism too often, too bluntly, too easily, and there is no point in making a long list of the Freudian images. A few examples will indicate the scope and intent. In *Give Your Heart to the Hawks* Michael slips a snake up the leg of Faye's blue-jeans. "That's to remember me by," he says. Other obviously phallic symbols appear in "Steelhead, Wild Pig, the Fungus" and in *The Women at Point Sur*. One may also find examples of the "unconscious" pun. The puns are not, however, all sexual, and one that comes to mind seems to me fairly successful. Vere Harnish (*The Double Axe*), contemplating the murder of her mother, says, as she jabs with a knife at a pelican that has crashed through the window in a storm, that the smell of the blood "mothers" her.

Freud's postulation of a form of infantile sexuality brings to mind Saint Augustine's question as to whether "this were the vaunted purity of childhood," and imparts a strange direction to the common romantic obsession with the child. The innocence is eroded, and only an eroded innocence, a sly epitome of evil may be found in the submerged entity to which the adult may under strain revert. In *The Coast-Range Christ* David Carrow deliriously dreams that he is a child again:

> Playing and wading along the sea-beach he found a cave among the rocks,
> Where he lay to watch his father plowing the field above, while flocks
> Of white sea-birds hovered plowman and horses and the happy and opened earth.
> *He* was hidden, he would delight in the cave, nothing should coax him forth.

Any—well, almost any—undergraduate could tell that Carrow's exhausted mind has turned to the protection of the womb. His reversion is loosely paralleled in the same poem when O'Farrell (the worldly man contrasted with Carrow) also dreams that he is a child:

> He was fishing from the bank, his sister barefoot to the lean knees
> Helped him when the line was tangled on a snag, then she went down
> Among quicksands, the quicksands murmured, "I am your mother, I am your own
> Mother and sister, prod me with your fishing-pole, we are down here,
> Waiting to be weighed from concealment . . . to be lifted in the wild air . . ."

Happily the motive of reversion is subtler in the later poem *Give Your Heart to the Hawks*. Driven to hysteria by guilt, Lance Fraser imagines himself a child again in a preguilt state, playing with his brother. But instead of the comatose rhetoric of *The Coast-Range Christ,* we have concreteness, colloquialism. Lance's speech is beautifully right:

> Mikey. Oh Mikey. Come home.
> I'll be *it* to-morrow again. It's getting too dark to play,
> Don't hide any more, buddy, for the owls are out.
> If you'll come in I'll let you have my cornelian,
> And the heron's eggs that I found.

But he is defeated in the attempt to re-create innocence, for suddenly he remembers an incident of impurity from his childhood: "Damned liar. Ma's not . . . mare. / People ain't made like . . . dirty . . ."

In *The Women at Point Sur* the implications of reversion to childhood become metaphysical. Barclay, as Jeffers tells us, harbors a covert desire for incest. He wishes to condone this desire and he tries accordingly to construct a God beyond good and evil who will sanction his deviation. The God he envisions is the amoral child, somewhat reminiscent of Mark Twain's mysterious stranger, "innocently laughing" at "war, torture, famine; oppressions; the secret cruelties; the plague in the air that killed its millions . . ." This God gives a fiat to every license and above all the license to break sexual taboo.

In the matter of sexual taboo, the impact of Freud is especially evident. In *Roan Stallion* and in the very passage where Jeffers for the first time formulates his Inhumanism, he mentions man's "wild loves that leap over the walls of nature." The reference is to a love of animals in this situation, but the "wild loves" which have most often leaped around in Jeffers' narratives are homosexuality and incest.

After April Barclay has been violated by her father,

her mind meanders in a reverie, a dream of adventure, of riding horses in Asiatic deserts. "These were new dreams and not a girl's dreams, an adolescent / Boy's, that made windy honey in her mind." Later when she gazes at the lesbians, Natalia Morhead and Faith Heriot, she changes "sex a moment." What had seemed repugnant to her in them becomes "the terrible beauty . . . The fury of archangelic passions . . ." It requires little ingenuity (and, I should say, not enough ingenuity) to gather that her father's violence has so shaken her that her sexual normalcy is wavering; she wishes to become male in order to defend herself against the male. This is a thesis which, in respect to the two lesbians, Jeffers takes pains to make precisely clear—as ludicrously clear, one may add, as a case history in a textbook. Faith Heriot, who assumes the active role in her relations with Natalia, has been deserted in an unmarried and pregnant state. Her mother obtains money from Faith's father for a cancer operation "in the same fountain" that is the source of Faith's trouble, but she gives the money to Faith for an abortion. When the father discovers what has occurred, he casts his daughter off. Afraid of her father, Faith goes her own way, finally falling exhausted outside Natalia's house. Natalia befriends her and eventually returns her love. Jeffers comments on his case history:

> Neither Natalia nor Faith
> Understood how the anguish of desertion, and the mother's sacrifice,
> The penalizing pain and weakness, had changed
> Faith's nature, who'd been punished not be caught twice,
> Not again suffer this misery. Drowned under consciousness
> That resolution: and furious envy of the man

The sex that only inflicted, not suffered: the tropic nature
Knowing that no fence would cage it found the other outlet.
She had found Natalia, young, hot, husband-forsaken,
Beautiful to be wooed: Faith had learned something
From school-girl friends in town, when her father kept the
        light at Point Pinos:
And the sweet furnace painted with natural friendship,
And at the furnace heart the jewel sterility,
The love without fear.

This, it seems to me, is taking the textbook with a vengeance, producing an impossibly mechanical motivation,
a flatness of statement where fiction, let alone poetry, simply
cannot survive.

The narratives after *The Women at Point Sur* are less
clinical, as may be observed in the treatment of lesbianism
in *Thurso's Landing*. As in *The Women at Point Sur* there
is a history of feminine reaction against male domination.
Haled back from her adulterous elopement, Helen Thurso
finds that the household now includes Hester Clark, a
mistress her husband has acquired during her absence.
Helen's attitude is one of sympathy up to a certain point.
She suggests that they run away together, promising that
she will work for her, beg for her, and "no disgust and no
bullying," but shortly she recoils, and her sympathy for
another woman who has suffered from masculine cruelty
transmutes to an active cruelty on her own part. She assumes the male role when, swimming with Hester, she
taunts and bullies her, at last carrying her ashore in her
arms. Although male homosexuality is central to *The
Cretan Woman* (1954), after *Thurso's Landing* (1932) Jeffers' interest is not detained by lesbianism. Incest as a symbol for "racial introversion," however, has endured.

Dr. Powell observed: "Incest as theme was used in *Californians* in a mild, Shelleyan way, but in the long narrative, *Tamar,* the Biblical story is transplanted and adapted in such realistic fashion as to frighten the timid."[6] I would reverse the observation. In "The Three Avilas," which Dr. Powell refers to in *Californians,* the brother-sister lovers are described thus:

> Shy in the sun, untamed and beautiful,
> Were they as the blue wave, but lovelier white.
> They seemed two wild white deer come down to cool
> Their autumn fever in the sea's delight.
> O, hidden above the cliff what leering-dull
> And viper-hateful eyes had impious sight
> Of bodies so divine—is even more hard
> And sour to tell than what was afterward.

The "viper-hateful eyes" belong to the sister's full brother (the lover is a half-brother), who, in what seems at least understandable disgust, is about to murder them both for their unnatural behavior. Probably unconsciously, however, the passage deifies the incestuous relationship, for it does not take much literary knowledge to detect the echoes from *Paradise Lost:* the incestuous lovers are presented as Adam and Eve, the righteous brother as Satan. The fascination with incest in "The Three Avilas" seems to me more distasteful than in *Tamar* for the reason that it is *not* turned to symbolical account. Even in *Tamar* the symbol is tentative, and it does not become formal until 1927 with the appearance of *The Women at Point Sur,* although *The Tower Beyond Tragedy* (1925) had moved in this direction. The theme does not appear again until *Such Counsels You Gave to Me* and *The Double Axe.* In these it is clear that the use is symbolical, but in each the motivation for incest is different. A Freudian explanation, reaction against the father, develops in *Such Counsels You Gave to Me* (1937). In *The Double Axe* (1948) the father is, to be sure, a brutal, insensitive person, but the motivation toward incest seems to depend more directly upon Hoult's exhaustion, which enforces a desire to return to the fountain of his being. He says that he is "lonely in pain." In the contrast between *Such Counsels You Gave to Me* and *The Double Axe* lies one of the unnoticed growths in Jeffers' poetry. It is a growth away from Freud, away from the clinical and toward the mystical.

3

As early as 1911 Carl Jung repudiated Freud's conclusions about the unconscious—particularly Freud's emphasis on the infantile and sexual nature of the unconscious drives. He did not at first differ radically and, indeed, embraced these emphases as being true of the neurotic state. His own interest, however, centered less and less in the neurotic and more in the normal person. Fairly early in his career he insisted:

The further development of mankind can only be brought about by means of symbols which represent something far in advance of himself, and whose intellectual meanings cannot yet be grasped entirely. The individual unconscious produces such symbols, and they are of the greatest possible value in the moral development of the personality.[7]

The statement looks forward to his theory of a "collective unconscious" with its Pelion of wonder heaped on its Ossa of mysticism. And Jeffers' ponderings since 1937 appear to me to have veered in the direction Jung has taken.

One of the residues of Jeffers' early fascination with
Shelley may be his subscription to the Zoroastrian notion
of an alter ego. In *The Women at Point Sur* Barclay meets
and argues with such a personage, to whom at one point he
mutters, "Here you are, madness. / The Magus Zoroaster
thy dead . . ." The phrase, "The Magus Zoroaster thy
dead," is excerpted from Shelley's *Prometheus Unbound,*
as Dr. Powell has pointed out. The passage in Shelley is
illuminating:

> *The Earth* [to Prometheus] . . . Ere Babylon was dust,
> The Magus Zoroaster, my dead child,
> Met his own image walking in the garden.
> That apparition, sole of men, he saw.
> For know there are two worlds of life and death:
> One that which thou beholdest; but the other
> Is underneath the grave, where do inhabit
> The shadows of all forms that think and live
> Till death unite them and they part no more;
> Dreams and the light imaginings of men,
> And all that faith creates or love desires,
> Terrible, strange, sublime and beauteous shapes.

May we suppose that Jeffers remembered and used a phrase
from this passage for the reason that it was consonant with
his own intuitions?

Alter egos appear in *Such Counsels You Gave to Me*
and *The Double Axe,* but in *Mara* (1941) the alter ego is
most elaborately developed. *Mara* opens with the protago-
nist face to face with his *Doppelgänger*. This self greets
Ferguson when, although "married to a beautiful girl, all
wants fulfilled . . . life in general looked dirty, senseless and
destitute." The wife, Fawn, emblematic of the moral dere-
liction which Jeffers associates with "civilization," seeks

and finds sexual variety in a secret affair with Ferguson's
brother Allen. Savoring a moral collapse all about him,
Ferguson casts about for some principle that will explain
what is happening to life, to society. He reads Spengler
and discovers what he thinks are "reasons." Against these
reasons, and also because of them, he tries to excuse his
wife's behavior on purely rational grounds: "Morality's
rooted / In religion, religion's hypnotic lies . . ." Like Barclay, he tries to escape moral responsibility, and truth "poisons" him. As a result of these strains, he seeks release in a
meaningless, drunken fight at a country dance; then, re-
fusing to ride with Fawn and Allen, he walks home. A
second apparition greets him on the walk. This time it is
not the alter ego of the opening passages of the poem but a
woman. She walks beside him on the road and says:

> "I have been here for years
> At the locked doors of your mind knocking . . ." "Go on,"
>   he said,
> "I'll believe anything." She said, "You used to want to
>   understand,
> You used to want to know the truth about things,
> And whether all this . . . immense establishment of earth
>   and stars,
> Flesh, mind and time and so forth has any purpose.
> But now you are lost in passion." "Hm? Not a bit. Pas-
>   sion? . . .
> Who are you anyway?" "Mara," she answered, but when
> He looked at her she was gone, and it seemed to him
> That he'd been talking to himself.

The word "Mara" is rich in allusion: the Irish goddess of
fate, "bitterness" in the Old Testament, a possessing spirit
in Nordic and Slavic mythology. And Mara is the name of

the god who tempts Buddha toward apathy when he is on the eve of delivering mankind, later tempting him toward self-extermination.

In later studies (antedating *Mara* by at least two years), Jung speaks of two aspects of the collective unconscious. These he calls the *anima* (or *animus*) and the "shadow." By the *anima* he means "the woman in man." By the shadow he means the masculine compulsion in the male's unconscious. The shadow, he holds, is "the inferior and less commendable" part, embracing "all those characteristics whose existence is painful or regrettable." The last observation is perhaps saddening since Jung further states that "meeting with oneself is the meeting with one's own shadow."

The *anima* in the male is the archetype of the eternal woman, creative, fruitful. Yet in certain aspects she "frequently stands for evil itself" and she may signify "the dreaded, dark, maternal womb, which is of ambivalent nature." Of the *anima* and the *animus* (the masculine archetype in the female's unconscious) Jung states:

They are masklike, wraithlike, without problems of their own or any self-reflection, with no conflict, no doubt, no suffering; something like the gods, who have no philosophy; like the Brahma-gods of the Buddhist Samyutta-nikāya whose erroneous views need Gautama Buddha's correction. They seem to be functions or instincts which appear in a personal form when aroused from their dormant condition. But contrary to the functions attached to consciousness, they are always strangers in the conscious world. Because they permeate the atmosphere with a feeling of uncanny foreboding, or even with the fear of mental derangement, they are unwelcome intruders.[8]

In *Mara* the parallels with Jung's theory are at least absorbing. The first alter ego (the "shadow"), we find, speaks to Bruce Ferguson in a "Hollow-chested voice like a consumptive's." This alter ego, we remember, is male, and like Jung's "shadow" has a thin, "inferior" quality. Also, when Ferguson descries the figure, he finds the "face was his own"; literally, then, a meeting with himself.

If the first apparition seems curiously similar to Jung's account of the "shadow," Mara appears in certain respects to parallel the characteristics of the *anima*. It may be only coincidence that "Mara" recalls the Buddhist legend; yet, if so, the neat harmony with Jung's phrase, "like the Brahma-gods of the Buddhist Samyutta-nikāya," would be strange. And certainly Mara fulfills the specifications of ambivalence and mystery which Jung outlines. We cannot be sure that her pronouncement is for better or worse, whether she represents the passions which she mentions or a release from passion. She inspires in Ferguson the fear of derangement that Jung also suggests may accompany her emergence into consciousness. And it is after meeting Mara that Ferguson commits suicide. One may, finally, compare Mara's vagueness and sinister ambivalence with Jung's ultimate assessment of the *anima:*

It is chaotic life-urge, to be sure, but something strangely meaningful also clings to it—something like secret knowledge or hidden wisdom, in most curious contrast to its irrational, elfin nature.[9]

At this point I want to make a generalization. Jeffers' narratives between *Tamar* (1924) and *Mara* (1941) are characterized by a Freudian scheme, with the result that the behavior of the characters is largely pseudo-naturalistic. They yearn toward incest; they revert to infantile dreams.

This is not the case with Bruce Ferguson. His struggle is not with a hidden impurity entombed in childhood; he struggles with the projections of his own personality.

The volume *Such Counsels You Gave to Me,* which precedes *Mara,* may in this respect be considered a transitional work, illustrating Jeffers' movement toward a Jungian formulation. Howard Howren also sees his shadowy alter ego at the beginning and at the end of the poem. The specter here is explicable in Freudian terms—hallucination as a result of hysteria—and yet the *function* of the shadow seems rather more Jungian. Howard's shadow mutters:

> My twenty years
> Of watching are at last ending. Why did you not
> Complete your cycle? You returned to the breasts of infancy,
> Not to the womb of birth.

Inasmuch as Howard Howren has just helped to murder his father and has verged upon committing incest with his mother, these words seem the sardonic, ambivalent laughter of the neutral gods.

The observable trend in both *Such Counsels You Gave to Me* and *Mara* is toward the mystical rather than the naturalistic, toward the Oriental rather than the Western, toward an identification of man with cryptic, divine archetypes rather than disconsolate mechanisms. The momentum of this trend seems to have impelled Jeffers beyond both Freud and Jung in *The Double Axe* and *Hungerfield* (1952), for while neurosis and violence recur, they appear in a framework of supernatural allegory which no recognizable psychology, no behavioristic philosophy conditions.

V

The Anatomy of Violence

The poets who sing of life without
remembering its agony
Are fools or liars.

Hungerfield

1

THE SINGLE MOST impressive characteristic of Jeffers' mature work is his preoccupation with all manner of violent action. The origins are not simple, but one can make inroads toward an understanding by considering the perplexing split between Jeffers' didacticism and its formulation. He arranges his characters so that they torture each other unbearably and then moralizes that if this is the human condition, it would be well to "break out" of it. He tries thus to solve the problem of passion through logic, but the effort augments his difficulties if only because it is man's irrational passions which most readily capture Jeffers' artistic allegiance.

This peculiar dichotomy (or should I say this common dichotomy of the twentieth century?) between the dictates of intellect and the pleas of passionate imagination gives us the portrait of a man who carefully gathers up dinner crumbs to scatter for the birds but who writes a sadistic poem about a mutilated hawk. One critic has confessed to the easy belief that Jeffers may be typed among "rigidly self-disciplined or timid persons who frequently revolt via their imaginations into the realms of violence." By a skillful misinterpretation of the poem "For Una" the same critic concludes that "Mr. Jeffers admits as much."[1] The principle of compensation probably operates to some degree in Jeffers' work, but one ought to be fearful of a current tendency to manipulate any psychological cause toward any convenient effect; and very careful about separating the artistic from the everyday personality.

The influence of the war is complicating. No violence appears in Jeffers' verse until after 1918. And more significantly, much of the violence in the poems can be taken as a symbol for war, even though the expression is often sexual. The identification, or at least the blurring in his work, of violence, war, and the passions is not superficial: For if Jeffers despises the brutality of war, he sometimes envisions war as an agency which, by humbling and upheaving, may create benefit. Likewise, if he seeks to deprecate the passions, he nevertheless envisions regeneration as the task of a primitive sexuality.

From his inability either to compose or ignore these conflicts, Jeffers has, I think, been forced to express them in an exaggerated form. When we regard the expression as half-deliberate exaggeration, we are in a position to estimate the relationship between the man and the violence which he has created. He does not, I suggest, turn to violence because his temperament longs for violence but because it longs to be rid of it. He seeks to destroy his own passions, along with the racial "passion" of war, by deliberately exaggerating them. We are reminded of what Yeats wrote about Oscar Wilde's behavior before his tragic collapse. All that "parade of gloom" and "that elaborate playing with tragedy," Yeats believed, "was an attempt to escape from an emotion by its exaggeration."[2]

This is as far as I can go with the problem of personality as such. It may, however, be that the remaining observations essentially are a description of personality, for although I relate the problem to theology, it is difficult to know if I am describing general formulas which the human psyche repeats as religious compulsions, or if I am describing the condition of one who, in repudiating formal religion, has guiltily magnified the vestiges of a creed.

Jeffers' early religious training was doubtless thorough, and probably not narrow. In a letter (1938) to Professor H. H. Waggoner, Jeffers stated: "My father was a clergyman but also intelligent."[3] William Hamilton Jeffers was more than a clergyman; he "was a distinguished theologian, the culmination of a long line of devout Calvinists."[4] Jeffers' feelings toward his learned father indicate a mixture of reverence and remorse. When his father died, Jeffers vowed to:

> Retrace his sacred footsteps reverently,
> And dream his life back to the power it was.

Twenty-five years later, Jeffers grieved:

> I dishonored and wasted all your hopes of me, one
> by one; yet I loved you well.

Is this tension of reverence and guilt the basis for Jeffers' Nietzschean concept of Christianity as a "strain"? The answer may lie in understanding the conflict between the old religious father and the agnostic son in *Give Your Heart to the Hawks*. Lance both revolts against the father who "spooned the gospel down my throat when I was a cub" and identifies himself with the father's gospel by dismissing mankind with the doctrine of original sin. Lance Fraser's dilemma is perhaps Jeffers' own. He rejects formal dogma but seems to stagger beneath the weight of a Calvinistic belief in the depravity of man.

Behind Calvin's credo stood an absolute trust in justice —reward by salvation or damnation in a life after death. No such faith exists for Jeffers. "We go down into blackness," Lance says. There is no permanently conscious immortality. Jeffers' idea of a hereafter is as dim and uncertain as Job's idea of Sheol, the shadowy limbo where identity dissolves. *Tamar* conspicuously and a number of the short poems contain ghosts who are in the process of fading. They exist for a time, as the stain of consciousness upon the inanimate universe, but they must, we are told, finally disintegrate. This final release from identity Jeffers upholds as man's great good fortune. Unlike Job, who contemplates the terrors of losing his sense of self and remains resolute against his wife's advice to "curse God, and die," Jeffers informs us that Madrone Bothwell in *Solstice* "had cursed God and lived."

Since for Jeffers there is no eternal life, no heaven nor hell, the perseverance of some sort of religious emotion demanding punishment for the original sin has had a profound effect upon his poetry. No more than the bewildered Job could expect reward in Sheol for his model conduct can Jeffers' characters, riddled with guilt, expect punishment for their crimes in an afterlife. Aware, then, of their guilt, they cry out for a fiery cleansing. The ghost of Helen in *Tamar,* knowing that she must dissolve into nothingness which cheats her of expiation, hisses, "There's no hell and curse God for it." Similarly, Cawdor, discovering that his son whom he has suspected of adultery and has murdered, is innocent of the crime, says that he would kill himself if he could believe in hell-fire. So terrible does his unabsolvable crime become to Cawdor that he permits himself to speculate vainly as to whether the son might have committed the crime if he had not watched him so carefully. He would choose to justify his own crime on the grounds of his son's capacity for sin, rather than dwell with his own, knowing that he cannot be cleansed by punishment.

One may well consider if this same attitude is not one of the reasons for the violence in Jeffers' narratives and dramas. To use the inverse parallel of Job again, one might judge that as Job must expect his reward in this life, so for Jeffers, punishment for sin must develop in this life. Certainly, the mental and physical torment which he delivers to his characters is scarcely exceeded by medieval descriptions of Satan's sadistic ingenuity. This demand for temporal punishment would seem to account for the recurrence again and again of brush and forest fires in the narratives, like the fires which mercifully terminate *Tamar,* the first part of *The Double Axe,* and *Hungerfield.*

2

Jeffers would appear to have taken justice into his own hands without precisely realizing his presumption. If he is induced to violence by his temperament, the inducement is reinforced by a religious intensity that demands punishment for universal guilt. We are especially aware of the violence, however, because without the purpose that a formal religion gives, all the punishment, truant and self-conscious, tends to assume the appearance of masochism: and this indictment is supported by the fundamental form—the torture of animals and of men—which punishment in Jeffers' poetry takes.

Except that a starving fawn is mentioned in *Californians,* the early poetry is free of tortured animals. As the implications, however, in Jeffers' universe intensified, his preoccupation with this motive grew. It is probably not important to erect a lurid zoo of unhappy beasts, but a few examples will not be insupportable. The most conspicuous are found in the two narratives *Cawdor* (1928) and *Give Your Heart to the Hawks* (1933). In the latter a Cooper's hawk with a broken wing is tethered by a cord to a peg and made to fight a game-cock:

> Lance pushed and freed the game-cock, that eagerly
> Staring-hackled in his battle-passion
> Leaped up and struck down; the hawk tripped by its wing
> Fell quivering under the spurs, but a long-fingered
> Lean yellow hand reaching up out of ruin
> Plucked at the red king's breast: who charged again: one
>   hawk-wing
> Waved, and the talons mysteriously accomplished
> Many quick bitter acts, whence the red king
> Reeled out of hope. He crouched beyond tether's reach,
> Propping himself on both wings, but the sinking head
> Still stretched for fight; then dull-eyed, at strength's end,
> Went staggering to it again. The yellow hands
> Easily made him what would never any more
> Chirp over bright corn to the hens or subdue a rival.
> Lance came, and the little hawk ran quickly and fell

> Onto its broken shoulder at the tether's end. Lance picked
>   up the dying game-cock;
> Red grains of wheat from the torn crop fell down with the
>   blood.

Such passages may easily seem introduced for the sake
of sensationalism. But the tortured animal plays a symbolic
role. This is made most clear in *Cawdor* where Michal
keeps as a pet a caged eagle which her brother Hood has
winged. In nearly two years of imprisonment the bird has
persisted in arrogant pride:

>   They stood and watched
> The dark square-shouldered prisoner, the great flight-feath-
>   ers
> Of the dragged wing were worn to quills, and beetles
> Crawled by the weaponed feet, yet the dark eyes
> Remembered their pride. Hood said "You ought to kill him.
> My God, nearly two years!" She answered nothing,
> But when he looked at her face the long blue eyes
> Winked and were brimmed. The grim hand took the squir-
>   rel,
> It made a whispering twitter, the bleak head tore it.

When the bird is finally put out of its misery Jeffers describes the flight of its "phantom" in one of his most successful pieces of writing, an elegy where death becomes an
affirmation of life:

>   There the eagle's phantom perceived
> Its prison and its wound were not its peculiar wretchedness,
> All that lives was maimed and bleeding, caged or in blind-
>   ness,
> Lopped at the ends with death and conception, and shrewd
> Cautery of pain on the stumps to stifle the blood, but not
> Refrains for all that; life was more than its functions

And accidents, more important than its pains and pleasures,
A torch to burn in with pride, a necessary
Ecstasy in the run of the cold substance,
And scape-goat of the greater world. (But as for me,
I have heard the summer dust crying to be born
As much as ever flesh cried to be quiet.)

Not only does this passage articulate a meaning of life, but
it also suggests that the eagle and his squalid cage are intended to symbolize the state of man, trapped in pain and
filth, but yet performing a "necessary" task in the universal
scheme. An earlier section of the same passage makes the
identification of the eagle and man more explicit, for the
phantom sees its own "archetype"—its god:

... according to the sight of its kind, the archetype
Body of life a beaked carnivorous desire
Self-upheld on storm-broad wings: but the eyes
Were spouts of blood; the eyes were gashed out; dark blood
Ran from the ruinous eye-pits to the hook of the beak
And rained on the waste spaces of empty heaven.

Like the eagle's god, Cawdor, too, in his cage of passions,
suspicion, and violence, takes the way of Oedipus, blinding
himself.

The tortured animal, then, is a symbol of man's plight.
But often the symbol is dropped, and man himself is tortured, principally in two patterns—castration and crucifixion. Old Morhead in *The Women at Point Sur* may be
taken as the prototype of the castrated man, but Reave in
Thurso's Landing is the more detailed example. He receives
the "hell of pain and impotence" in an accident which in
itself voices the failure of mankind. In *Give Your Heart to
the Hawks* Lance Fraser, only temporarily impotent and

for psychological reasons, embodies both the castration motive and that of crucifixion. Suffering the pangs of conscience, he rakes his hands across a barbed wire fence so "that the barbs of the wire clicked on the bones of his hands through the torn flesh." Obviously a simulation of the wounds of Christ. Later these wounds become infected, and losing his reason, he commits suicide. Bruce Ferguson too, in *Mara,* under a different strain, cuts his hands just before he takes his own life.

It is noteworthy that in these two narratives, where the disease of life becomes especially painful, self-crucifixion is the forerunner of insanity and suicide. In this way the Christ-figure is related to the insanely self-tortured man. And Jeffers takes the relationship one step further by relating the Christ-figure to war. The whole process of symbolic thought whereby Jeffers moves from the tortured animal to man, thence to Christ, and finally to war as a vast, ceaseless process of self-torture is condensed in one passage in *Such Counsels You Gave to Me.* Howard Howren dreams:

> That he and others in the laboratory were nailing a dog to
>   wings, driving sharp horse-shoe nails
> Between the pads of the fore-paws into the shafts of the
>   wing-frames. The dog vanished from the dream, the
>   dreamer
> Himself flying wide over the city, crucified to wings; one of
>   the spikes tore out through his palm
> And he pitched down, falling along the façade of a public
>   building.

Christ and war interweave in Jeffers' thought, but for the moment let us consider them separately. War, to Jeffers, is the absolute in man's folly. His statements, however, in this regard being elusive, led Hildegarde Flanner in 1937 to observe that ". . . he has recommended war, the cruelest of man's manias, as a way of cleansing civilization and leading life back to reality."⁵ It is hard to say that the critic has been entirely misled, yet it would be wrong to say that the insight is entirely right. Jeffers has sometimes tried to find some meaning in war, but the meaning has always been the long-range one, the shadowy contours in the Spenglerian vista. War, Jeffers sometimes sees as the inevitable trap but never as the desirable course for man in a high state of civilization. On the contrary, war becomes the focal point of his diatribes against mankind. It can only end "in horror," he says. Indeed, the human body is "essentially unwarlike," and man makes a fool of himself in war. In *The Double Axe* his invective against war reaches a culmination in the characterization of Hoult Gore, who is the epitome of the crucified man. Killed in a Pacific (unhappy irony!) battle, by power of will he drags his corpse back to his home. War has left him with the desire to kill needlessly, and he murders his father as a "war monger." But Hoult must be seen, too, as a personification of Western civilization. His "corpse," he says, "covers the western world and sprawls over Asia." The characterization allows us now to reconsider Jeffers' unconventional conjunction of the Christ-figure and war. Hoult, the corpse of the Western world, parodies the sacrament, drawing an obscene caricature of a dying soldier, which he gives to his mother and father, saying:

> Now it is comic. Take it in remembrance of me. This is my body
> That was broken for nothing. Drink it: this is my blood

That was spilled for no need. Oh, yes: for victory:
That rat-sucked hawk-egg.

It is time to ask, why this identification of Christ and
war? The drama *Dear Judas* is the logical place to look for
the answer. Here Christ deliberately chooses crucifixion as
a means to power. To Judas his decision is one that will
bring twenty centuries of war. He says to Jesus, "To let the
people alone is mercy: all stirring is death to them." And in
"The Theory of Truth" Jeffers writes:

> The beautiful young poet found truth in the desert, but
> found also
> Fantastic solution of hopeless anguish. The carpenter was
> not his father? Because God was his father,
> Not a man sinning, but the pure holiness and power of God.
> His personal anguish and insane solution
> Have stained an age; nearly two thousand years are one
> vast poem drunk with the wine of his blood.

I am anxious to confess that so far I have offered a one-
sided picture of the Christ-war motive. The essential attitude is not simplex. Indeed, a deep-rooted ambivalence is
hinted at in the phrasing of the passage above and openly
documented in the short poem "The Redeemer," which
presents a man who thinks he is saving the world by keep-
ing old wounds in his palms fresh; he is insane, but it is
clear that Jeffers thinks him not merely harmlessly mad
but also divinely so. In another poem of about the same
time Jeffers admits that he once considered becoming a
"savior" in order to bring "peace to the unborn children,"
but he concludes that it is unnecessary because death is a
final savior.[6] After a brief excursion in another direction I
shall return to this problem.

3

There are two extensions to Jeffers' religious intensity: his attitude toward the phenomenon of consciousness, and his misogyny.

In the poem "Margrave" (1932) Jeffers implies that the dissolution of consciousness is not without compensation. Of course, the oriental concept of nirvana comes to mind. Amos Wilder has written of this aspect of the poetry,[7] and Rudolph Gilbert mentions traces of Sufism.[8] My impression is that, while Jeffers has undoubtedly absorbed oriental philosophy, his aspersions about consciousness may be elucidated within the framework of Christian theology. At this point a parallel with Milton pleads for expression.

Milton's purpose in *Paradise Lost* was to preach absolute reason and a merciful God, but his preoccupation in detail was with the nature of sin. The justification for bringing the humanist and the inhumanist together resides in Milton's propagation of a patristic (ultimately Saint Augustine's) reasoning to the effect that the origin of sin is pride, the conscious turning from God to self. Such is Satan's archetypal sin, and it is shared by Eve. Describing her first hours on earth, she tells of wandering toward the "murmuring sound" of water and coming to a "smooth lake." Here she relates:

> ". . . I bent down to look, just opposite
> A shape within the watery gleam appeared
> Bending to look on me: I started back,
> It started back, but pleased I soon returned,
> Pleased it returned as soon with answering looks
> Of sympathy and love; there I had fixed
> Mine eyes till now, and pined with vain desire,

Had not a voice thus warned me. 'What thou seest,
What there thou seest, fair creature, is thyself . . .' "

On the reverse side of the manuscript of *The Tower Beyond Tragedy* Jeffers once copied out this passage with the comment that it was an example of "narcissism," a view which C. S. Lewis twenty years later came to hold. Jeffers, it is true, questions not merely self-consciousness, the "bosom serpent" of Hawthorne, but the whole fact of consciousness. Yet his reason—that the consciousness turns to itself rather than to God—is the patristic reason.

Milton also gives an insight into the related problem of Jeffers' misogyny. His urgency to demonstrate both God's capacity for mercy and man's capacity for sin forced Milton to show that the Adamic side of mankind is superior to Satan; otherwise, why should man be saved at all? At the same time, Milton had to account for the fall without permitting Adam to sink to the level of Satan. Hence it is Eve who, like Satan, is the narcissist; and Eve who commits the Satanic sin of self-consciousness and then disobedience. Adam's weakness is simply his love for another human being. He slides down with Eve, but it is only the female half of the race that has originated the sin.

Jeffers' heroines frequently undermine the nobility of his heroes; they are narcissistic Eves. Fawn in *Mara,* for example, strokes "herself with her hands / Lovingly." These heroines are hectic in their disregard for conventional morality. Fickle, lascivious, Tamar and Electra argue seductively for incestuous unions, as do the mothers in *Such Counsels You Gave to Me, The Double Axe,* and *The Cretan Woman.* Female promiscuity underlies the tragedies in *Thurso's Landing, Cawdor, Give Your Heart to*

the Hawks, and *Mara.* And though his heroes are power-
less to change the heroines or their world, they are aware
of their own superior natures. Lance Fraser asks of Fera,
"Did y' love him? Or was it only because you're female
. . . female and drunk?"

4

I have related Jeffers' symbol of the tortured man to a
religious intensity, and I have suggested that there is a connection between his attitude toward consciousness and a
theological tradition. I wish that the whole scheme were
more free of inconsistency, but to some extent the confusions are tidied, the conflicts reconciled in Jeffers' concept of
God.

During the course of Jeffers' career his God has
changed from the wild god of Nature incarnate in the roan
stallion that shakes "the red-roan mane for a flag on the
bare hills," to a more nearly intelligent God in *The Double
Axe.* The later figuration is that of Heautontimoroumenos,
the self-tormentor, first hinted at in "Apology for Bad
Dreams." In the image of the self-tormenting God, Jeffers
cautiously narrows the gap between man and Nature. But
he does not close it entirely. For the inevitable question
arises: If God is a self-tormentor, tormenting himself for
the purpose of discovery, why does Jeffers rail at man's self-
torture, his crucifixions, his wars? The answer lies in the
disparity between divine and human intention. God's torment is not "cruel," it is necessary to knowledge. Human
perpetration of cruelty, however, is a different matter. Jeffers would have man suffer the pangs of tragic discovery
but he would have him eschew the perversion of a pointless
sadism:

> Man's world is a tragic
> music and is not played for man's happiness,
> Its discords are not resolved but by other discords.
>
> But for each man
> There is real solution, let him turn from himself and man
> to love God. He is out of the trap then. . . .
> But how could I impart
> this knowledge . . .?
>
> I know that
> all men instinctively rebel against it. But yet
> They will come to it at last.
> Then man will have come of age; he will still suffer and
> still die, but like a God, not a tortured animal.[9]

And this is the important difference: to suffer "like a God, not a tortured animal," for this illumines the whole of Jeffers' scheme, revealing why the tortured animals are an elemental necessity to his negative didacticism. Man may suffer like God, but since man cannot become God, the tragedies of life are only a reflection of celestial tragedy; man's tortures are a dream in Nature, while God's tortures are "in earnest,"[10] meaningful, infinite. Within these relationships Jeffers reconciles his simultaneous love and hatred of violence: the "love" on the grounds that violence is a divine activity, the "hate" on the grounds that it is too often a human perversion.

On similar premises Jeffers clarifies his distrust of human consciousness. But the distrust needs clarifying, for if pursued to the ultimate, his doubt denies the very reasoning which provides him with his conclusion. Yet, just as there is a divine self-torment, so there is a divine consciousness:

A conscious God?—The question has no importance. But
   I am conscious: where else
Did this consciousness come from? Nobody that I know of
   ever poured grain from an empty sack.
And who, I would say, but God, and a conscious one,
Ended the chief war-makers with their war, so humorously,
   such accurate timing, and such
Appropriate ends? The man of vanity in vanity,
Having his portrait painted; the man of violence . . . in
   the fire and frenzy
Of Berlin falling.[11]

Hence consciousness is only evil when it is diverted by the
man of vanity from God, and pointless human violence inevitably turns back upon the violent human being.

    It remains to observe that Christ, the titan who
"brought fire to his tribe," has also a place, intellectually
conceived and reconciled, within the system. As the hanged
god of Norse mythology in *At the Birth of an Age,*
Christ says:

My truth is born. It has nothing to do with the dead; I loved
   the living and taught them to love each other.
Even now on earth my love makes war upon death and
   misery, not like a sword, like a young seed,
And not men's souls, but far down the terrible fertile future
   their children, changed and saved by love,
May build the beauty of an earthly heaven on all our dead
   anguishes, and living inherit it.

The hope thus which Christ offers is mortal happiness, not
immortal glory. Yet as an intensification of man's desire to
emulate the self-torturing God, Christ has greater understanding of the divine pattern:

>   Every discovery
>   is a broken shield, a new knife of consciousness
> Whetted for its own hurt; pain rises like a red river: but also
>   the heroic beauty of being,
> That all experience builds higher . . .
>   These are my mercy and my
>   goodness, these
> My peace. Without the pain, no knowledge of peace,
>   nothing. Without the peace,
> No value in the pain. I have long strength.

By a devious path Christ comes to his traditional office; He interprets and evaluates pain and experience; He connects man and God.

A final question remains: Is life, either for God or man, only alternations of pain and peace, a series of hot and cold seizures? Perhaps. But I interpret Jeffers as saying that these two states are ultimately synthesized in the dimension of God. When the eagle in *Cawdor* released its phantom, fierce, arrogant bird that it is, it left "life behind," and

> The great unreal talons took peace for prey
> Exultantly, their death beyond death; stooped upward, and
>   struck
> Peace like a white fawn in a dell of fire.

The white fawn is Jeffers' symbol for supernatural beauty, the reality behind appearance. One must find even this final beauty in the heart of fire. Yet this is not the fire of violence, torture, punishment, but the fire of God, which preserves rather than scourges.

VI

The Eternal Peasant

1

FROM THE OPENING of any of the narratives it is clear that Jeffers is deeply interested in the behavior of people whose passions are hasty and clumsy and whose experience is limited to rather elemental discoveries. I have somewhat arbitrarily assigned the term "primitivism" to this predilection. Obviously, I am using the term in a much more general way than does Yvor Winters, who states that a "primitive poet is the major poet on a smaller scale."[1]

One of the continuing characteristics of American literature has been its eagerness to acknowledge or to repudiate the frontier. The acknowledgment has taken different forms: the daring, chaotic speculation of Whitman or Melville, the local color of Mark Twain or Sarah Orne Jewett, the belligerent regionalism of the stories about Mike Fink. At the core of any very self-conscious regionalism dwells a distrust of the city, a disdain, like Huckleberry Finn's, for "civilization." The established community is considered effeminate, whereas the frontier outpost is held masculine and vigorous.

Something of this regional feeling appears in Jeffers' poetry. He is writing "west of the west," he advises us in the "Epilogue" to *Flagons and Apples*. In "Maldrove" (*Californians*) the "mother-country" represents a primal beauty with which only the primitive mind can reckon. Man himself has become inadequate to the "mother-country," and so the poet must create "lovely and great sons" as "successors of these little verminous ones" to people the mighty region.

In the work following *Californians* Jeffers set himself the task of creating characters as primitive as the country which his imagination urged his eyes to see. But though he promised to create titans worthy of the last frontier, his Spenglerian loyalties made that aim ultimately impossible. It would, to be sure, have been feasible to write, like some of the Victorians, of a time as remote as the Middle Ages or the Italian Renaissance and hence to elude the difficulties of his own time, but Jeffers wanted his poetry to be of this age, while aimed at no age. Even when adapting material from Aeschylus or Euripides he has slanted the implications toward modern society. And since these implications derived from Spengler, his characters are montages, their primitive natures shadowed by a deteriorating culture. In notes written on the reverse side of the manuscript of *The Tower Beyond Tragedy,* Jeffers told himself that his characters had to partake both of the permanent world of Nature and of the transient world of man.[2] But being aware of a problem and solving it are two different things: characters in real life are seldom both decadent and primitive. Jeffers tried to solve the problem by splitting most of his characters into dual symbols for the antitheses which pre-occupied him: impotence and fecundity; decay and growth; decadence and primitivism. His characters behave *symbolically* like primeval savages but they fall *symbolically* into the snares of civilization. As bifocal symbols the inhabitants of his narratives achieve what he wanted them to, but all too often, lacking simple, human reality, they fail to convince the reader that they are characters. This is not so serious a flaw in poetry as it would be in prose but it is nevertheless a fault. We are more sympathetic to Jeffers' dilemma as an artist than we are to the dilemma of his characters.

In directing attention to regionalism and the Spenglerian mood, I have touched on what I think are the most immediate and important foundations of Jeffers' brand of primitivism. But there are other elements affecting Jeffers, along with other modern primitivists. First off, it goes without saying that a re-creative primitivism recurs throughout literature, and in post-Renaissance literature a fairly definite line runs from Mrs. Behn to Wordsworth. This is a line wherein the primitivism is entirely rational. Wordsworth's sallies of "imagination" do not disturb the central province of his faith in reason. But once faith in reason began to wither, the line turned in a different direction.

Against the rational constructs of the late eighteenth century arose the antirational expression of Nietzsche's disillusionment with the humanistic tradition. It had failed, this tradition, failed utterly for him. He had to transvalue values, and the way he set about doing so was by kicking at the posts of Christian humanism, at Christianity itself, and at social reforms which reflect an application of the Christian ideal. He fed the resultant vacuum with a neo-primitivism based not on any rational concept but on an irrational supposition which effloresced in *The Birth of Tragedy*. Essentially he argued that if the tradition of reason had not succeeded in realizing the potential greatness of man, then one should start again, this time from an anti-humanistic and antirational basis. Spengler, confessing that he owed "practically everything" to Nietzsche (but also to Goethe), yielded to a faith in "the eternal peasant." And Nietzsche (who was among the first—and perhaps the most important of all—to emphasize the dark, unaccountable impulses, and who saw danger in subduing this dark side) watered with his disillusionment the roots of Freud's and Jung's psychology.

In returning briefly to Freud and Jung I am primarily pondering the possible effects of their conclusions on a literary awareness. As to Freud, any such effect derives from the aura of suggestion. In his studies of totem and taboo Freud implies that primitive races lived closer to a natural morality, where the compulsion toward certain religious crimes (particularly incest) was more successfully controlled by primitive taboo than by the codes of modern society. I do not suppose that this moralistic overtone is part of Freud's intent. He was concerned pre-eminently with suggesting that taboos arise in primitive races because a compulsion toward perversity exists in primitive man and that therefore this same compulsion exists in modern man. Yet the effect of this reasoning on a mind like Jeffers' or, say, D. H. Lawrence's, might be that of fostering a didactic primitivism, for it would seem, after all, that it is modern, civilized man who is driven to imbalance by the quarrel between compulsion and conscience—not the savage.

To Freud the savage instinct was something to be reckoned with but it remained a savage instinct, and primitive man was interesting to him primarily as an ontogenetic explanation of contemporary man. The nature of primeval man corresponds in Freud's studies with the nature of the child in a civilized state. But for Jung the primal urges remain in themselves important, emphatically so; for the collective unconscious with its insistence on archetypal images is represented as a source of creative energy, the very "foundation" on which the personal consciousness is built. He everywhere discovers the savage breaking through into the civilized psyche, not merely in dreams but in alchemical symbols and poetry as well. Nor is the presence of this savage necessarily an *ignis fatuus,* leading one to the abyss; it may be a genuine illumination which can help one to discovery and fulfillment. This aspect of Jung's thought— which may well seem an ornamented form of the Christian notion of being led by a little child—grants power and superlative value to man's childlike past, but it subjects his reason to his imagination, and his imagination to possession by phantoms.

A distinct yet parallel drift toward primitivism occurs in literature, appearing, curiously enough, in a dubious form in Walter Pater. Yet perhaps it is not entirely curious, for in the cases of Nietzsche and Spengler it is precisely at the point where faith in the humanistic tradition perishes that one discovers a preoccupation with primitivism. I do not mean to imply that Pater abandoned humanistic learning. The opposite is true. I refer to his losing the meaning of humanistic learning in his subjective impressionism, and to the appearance at the very edge of attenuation of the sly beginnings of a primitivism. It is concealed, to be sure, staring up like the eye of a monster from the mud at the bottom of a placid pool. But it is there, and the form which it takes is a reactivation of diabolic paganism. In the whole scope of his work, Pater's restored Apollo and Dionysos are curiosities, and one would be tempted to dismiss them except that they accurately foreshadow the course of a primitivism oddly entangled with demonism in the present century.

It is convenient to make the usual observation that Pater's direction toward enervation continues in Oscar Wilde. The demonism reappears, too, in the silly figure of Dorian Gray. It reappears even more tangibly in the work of Arthur Machen. Machen, sometimes a good, sometimes a very bad, writer, represents a queer mixture of primitivism and decadence in his stories about the "little people." His male characters demonstrate the same interest in exotic vintages and the sordid districts of London as does Wilde's prince of darkness. At the same time, a consistent theme runs through his stories, the theme of an approach to "the great god Pan" by way of an exhausting, somewhat masochistic identification of self with Nature. In essence the theme falters toward primitivism, although, as in the later expression of James Branch Cabell, one does not expect it to falter very far. The motive, however, flowers in the demonic primitivism of D. H. Lawrence.

2

Something of a Jeffers cult thrived with the Lawrence cult in Taos, New Mexico, during the 1930's. The extraordinary Dorothy Brett called her house in Taos "The Tower Beyond Tragedy," and Mabel Dodge Luhan addressed her book on Lawrence to Jeffers. The book begins:

You know, Jeffers, after I met you, I felt that you and Lawrence ought to know each other, that you would have liked and understood each other; and I asked you to give me the two books of poems to send to him, and to write something in one of them especially for him. . . . Then, before they ever reached him, just in those two weeks, he was dead—and now you will never meet.[3]

I think the two of them might have liked each other, but I am not convinced that they would have understood each other. Nevertheless, they do have much in common. As others have pointed out, there is a notable coincidence in the fact that Jeffers' study of a woman's love for a horse, *Roan Stallion,* appeared the same year (1925) as Lawrence's similar novelette *St. Mawr,* while *Dear Judas* (1929) was written at about the same time as Lawrence's treatment of Christ in *The Escaped Cock,* later entitled *The Man Who Died.*[4] And it goes without saying that both Jeffers and Lawrence evince the deepest interest in the primal aspects of life.

The emergence of primitivistic motives in Lawrence and Jeffers is the direct result of their catching a whiff of decay on the wind. Like Edna St. Vincent Millay, Hart Crane, and F. Scott Fitzgerald, they had read and, with different intensities, approved of Spengler's hypothesis. Crane, though a fine poet, wanted education and intellectual endurance; he could read and believe Spengler without its having any profound effect upon him. Fitzgerald and Millay treed the contemporary mood by turning its own cynicism and despair upon itself, while Jeffers and Lawrence turned the mood loose among humorless symbols set up in reaction to the supposed decadence. Lawrence thought of the decadence in terms which are not greatly at odds with Jeffers'. In *St. Mawr* Lou, the heroine, has a vision of cancerous evil:

And it had swept mankind away without mankind knowing. It had caught up the nations as the rising ocean might lift
the fishes, and was sweeping them on in a great tide of evil.[5]

But if the vision of evil was similar, the response to that
vision was not.

Lawrence felt that surely behind the drapery of modern man stood a strapping, sensual pagan who could be
drawn forth, and, once drawn forth, could heal the modern
disease. What most interfered with the emergence of the
pagan virtues was, Lawrence felt, an imbalance and deterioration in the relationship of the sexes. Man and wife had
become "pals" and in so doing had lost some mysterious
dignity, some inexplicable magic and power. In the *Fantasia of the Unconscious* he rails against this deterioration,
enjoining husbands to reassert (in a psychic rather than
purely sexual sense) their virility. In all reality, however,
the emphasis is neither psychic nor sexual but demonic.
Devil-worship recurs, of course, through much of Lawrence's writing, but in *The Plumed Serpent* (1926) it comes
to a head. The heroine, identifying herself with an Aztec
goddess, is reborn as Mexico is reborn, in the resurrection of
the old gods. Her lover's manhood, we are told, is "like
a devil inside of" him, and his face "the face at once of a
god and a devil, the undying Pan face." And this atavistic
diabolism rather clearly separates Lawrence's primitivism
from Jeffers'. Tamar, it is true, is violated during the orgi-
astic séance by "dead Gods," but Tamar is hardly to be
associated with virtue or vigor. Elsewhere Jeffers takes the
trouble to inform us that he has "never mistaken / Demon
. . . for the real God."[6]

There is another significant difference: With that immense faith in life that only dying men seem to achieve, Lawrence could accept the gloomy speculations of Spengler and still feel that civilization as the expression of life itself possessed a quality of continuity. He could admit that things were bad, but

> ... this time, it seems to me, we have consciously and responsibly to carry ourselves through the winter-period, the period of death and denudation: that is, some of us have, some *nation* even must. For there are not now, as in the Roman times, any great reservoirs of energetic barbaric life.[7]

And this is characteristic of Lawrence's thought. He could not put his chips on the rise of some future civilization. He felt that he could activate the Dionysian mystery in his own life and perhaps in the lives of others—maybe even in the drabbest working man's, of whom he wrote: "I would like to save him alive, in his living, spontaneous, original being. I can't help it. It is my passionate instinct."[8] But for Jeffers, even though the individual is not compelled to be corrupt by the corruption of his age, there can be no immediate solution. History must run its course through a long future period of tension and decline; there is no other way. Jeffers was sensible of this difference. Of *The Plumed Serpent* he said, "... I can believe of Lawrence wanting to revive the dead gods, but I can't believe it of Mexicans!"[9] And in the foreword to a posthumous volume of Lawrence's poems he comments:

> I think of Lawrence as the last Protestant. His earnestness and missionary zeal, his quest of salvation, his sacrifice of dignity, his faith in intuition, the inner guidance—he called it sometimes 'thinking with the blood,' others have called it inspiration by the Holy Ghost,—his distrust of establishments

and institutions, even his penetration into the dark corners of psychology:—all these are the powerful qualities of early Protestantism. But this is Protestantism far gone in decline; it retains its energies and has lost its direction. Bunyan was entirely sure of the means of salvation; Lawrence wished to be sure, often convinced himself that he was sure. The prescription was on the tip of his tongue; but it was hard to formulate, and it waned from time to time.

·   ·   ·   ·   ·   ·   ·   ·   ·   ·   ·   ·   ·

Lawrence went about the world looking for that lost clue to the labyrinth; perhaps it was in Asia, perhaps the Buddhists in Ceylon had it—but no! they were worse than the Christians. . . . Last, in his best poem ["The Ship of Death"], he began to consider the Egyptians . . . he never found what he sought; but his work, and in some degree his genius were produced by that febrile search.

And who has ever found the magical faith or magical knowledge, on which to build a new culture? I think of one example: the early Christians did. But they did not know it, nor even imagine such a thing. They were not preparing for a new age, but for the end of the world.[10]

Like Lawrence, Jeffers was stimulated by his stay at Taos to consider the relationship of modern man to his primitive origins; he came to a conclusion emphatically different from that to be found in *The Plumed Serpent:*

I watch the Indians dancing to help the young corn at Taos
    pueblo. The old men squat in a ring
And make the song, the young women with fat bare arms,
    and a few shame-faced young men, shuffle the dance.

·   ·   ·   ·   ·   ·   ·   ·   ·   ·   ·   ·

These tourists have eyes, the hundred watching the dance,
    white Americans, hungrily too, with reverence, not
    laughter;

Pilgrims from civilization, anxiously seeking beauty, religion, poetry; pilgrims from the vacuum.

People from cities, anxious to be human again. Poor show
how they suck you empty! The Indians are emptied,
And certainly there was never religion enough, nor beauty
nor poetry here . . . to fill Americans.[11]

Clearly, then, Jeffers would avoid superstition and fad. But
what does he seek to encounter?

Primitivism, in the sense of strong sexuality, fascinated
Jeffers early in his career because, as he wrote, ". . . the
sexual beauty of a man or woman is a token and advertise-
ment of racial permanence."[12] This is the feeling which
pervades "Fauna" and "The Maid's Thought," both written
somewhat earlier than *Tamar*. The feeling does not ever
entirely disappear from his work, but as his attack upon
man intensified, it in part took the form of attacking him
on the grounds of sexual license, so that, beginning with
Tamar, the "sexual beauty" is soured by being the source of
sorrow and evil. This is all too obviously a contradiction in
Jeffers' work.

I have already mentioned another contradiction;
namely, that his Carmel peasants are not simplex primi-
tives. Forgetting their lamination, however, we may take
them as Jeffers' deliberate rejection of urbanity—he wishes
to write of the effects of civilization but not of its appearance. When we enter the minds of his characters we are in
the vaults of bedlam, and the madness is symptomatic of
Jeffers' judgment of the modern world. But when we look
at their passionate spirit and physical power we see Jeffers'
conception of the eternal peasant. So, with Lance Fraser
in *Give Your Heart to the Hawks:*

> He was like this mountain coast,
> All beautiful, with chances of brutal violence; precipitous,
>   dark-natured, beautiful; without humor, without ever
> A glimmer of gayety; blind gray headland and arid moun-
>   tain, and trailing from his shoulders the infinite ocean.

Perhaps Madrone Bothwell in *Solstice* is a unified, primitive character. All her force is arrayed against civilization, against the encroachment of the city on her and her children. When she is told that she must leave her house because her former husband plans to make it into a tourist's resort, she comments, "A stew-pot for nature- / Lovers and sick drunkards." She kills her children rather than expose them to the "advantages" which the former husband plans to give them: "radio, motion-pictures, books / The school, the church." When she escapes into the desert, and Jeffers wishes to preserve the essential meaning of her character, we are told that she waits for civilization to die:

> Troublesome, contemptuous, archaic, with thunderstorm
>   hair and snowline eyes, *waiting,*
> Where the tall Rockies pasture with their heads down,
>   white-spotted and streaked like piebald horses, sharp
>   withers
> And thunder-scarred shoulders against the sky, standing
>   with their heads down, the snow-manes blow in the
>   wind;
> But they will lift their heads and whinny when the riders
>   come, they will stamp with their hooves and shake
>   down the glaciers.

Well, if Madrone Bothwell is up there waiting in the Rockies, she is no doubt more comfortable as a pure symbol than as a real character. One was never required, after all, to take her personality very seriously. But one must take

Medea, for whom Madrone Bothwell is but preparation, quite seriously.

The structural changes which Jeffers imposes on Euripides' play in the interest of modern theatre are minor. The chorus is muted, and Jeffers abandons the questionable action of Medea's escaping in a celestial chariot at the end of the play. But the changes in psychological motivation are sweeping.

Euripides portrayed a middle-aged Jason who, finished with the arduous adventures of youth, deserts Medea and her two sons to make an advantageous marriage with the daughter of Creon, king of Corinth. Medea takes vengeance by killing Creon and his daughter through sorcery and then murdering her sons. The bereft Jason is left with his rotting ship, Argo. Euripides balanced the evil of Jason's injustice against the evil of Medea's barbarousness. Jeffers' adaptation allows major shifts of emphasis. Medea, for whom Euripides apologized by saying that she behaves as no Greek woman would, in Jeffers' treatment becomes the primitive par excellence. Her behavior evolves as the inevitable result of her uneven union with Jason. She is a woman of primeval passions—Jason is worldly, ambitious; and the tragedy develops from the contrast between her warmth, his coldness; her naturalness, his opportunistic realism; her primitive spirit and his civilized urbanity. Where Euripides apologizes, Jeffers reveres. And so the play unfolds as the triumph of the primitive spirit over civilization:

> . . . I, a woman, a foreigner, alone
> Against you and the might of Corinth—have met you
> throat for throat, evil for evil. Now I go forth

Under the cold eyes of the weakness-despising stars:—not
me they scorn.

It is noteworthy that Jeffers' primitive characters seldom, however, triumph over *modern* civilization. Maruca,
the Indian woman in *The Women at Point Sur,* for example, is no doubt intended to suggest the permanence of
Nature. Her oppressive femaleness "suffocates" Barclay,
and at the end we are told that she carries a wild Christ in
her womb. But, like Madrone Bothwell, Maruca is not a
character in a story. She is perhaps a figure in anthropo-
logical history. Jeffers does not mean that an actual Maruca will or can bring about a renascence at Point Sur,
but only that eventually renascence takes place in the course
of Nature's will. Similarly, Fayne Fraser in *Give Your
Heart to the Hawks* claims to carry the world's savior in her
womb. Some have, on this evidence, felt that Jeffers is offer-
ing Fayne's faith as his own, that he is finishing up on a note
of hope.[13] In an extended sense, the historical sense, he is.
But Jeffers has little sympathy for Fayne's creed. Her husband has committed the crime of Cain, and she pleads with
him to trample the laws of society, to give his heart to the
hawks. If she were successful, one might be obliged to suppose that Jeffers derives directly from Nietzsche. But she is
not. Lance Fraser obtains salvation not by going beyond
good and evil but by recognizing good and evil, by rejecting Fayne's advice and neutralizing his sin in suicide. Fayne
is an example not of triumphant primitivism but of the
irony of attempting to behave like a primitive in the present
age. For, indeed, Jeffers, though a faithful primitivist in
the long view, does not want primitivism to conquer civilization, but civilization to conquer itself.

These are the boundaries, then, of Jeffers' "natural philosophy." He presents it as an energy which has meaning primarily in historical application. Unlike Lawrence, he does not advocate attempting to nourish the demonic talents of the psyche. He may admire and long for a primitive rejuvenation, but he cannot argue for something which he cannot visualize as attainable in a state of high civilization. For Jeffers the primitive force of life is present primarily in the symbol. Yet for that very reason it is powerfully omnipresent. He may have his immediate doubts about mankind, but he has no doubts about the pattern Nature will describe. The dog, Snapper, in *The Double Axe* may become too domestic, too civilized and begin, as the old man says, "to stink a little," but eventually she mates with a wolf. The old man calmly observes:

> She has been a traitress, and in spring she'll drop wolf-cubs.
> The world reverts. Dogs and men tire of a slow decline.

Lawrence would not have thought the dog a traitress.

VII

The Inhumanist

1

SURVEYING THE "unhappy time" of the late 1930's, Robinson Jeffers in an unusually compassionate mood told a world that was faltering toward war:

> I wish you could find the secure value,
> The all-heal I found when a former time hurt me to the heart,
> The splendor of inhuman things: you would not be looking at each others' throats with your knives.[1]

The "all-heal" Jeffers came eventually to call "Inhumanism." He has offered a number of depositions in poetry and prose to define his belief, but before examining them it is well to scrutinize what may be taken as the basic expression in *Californians* (1916), a volume where he seldom had his guard up. Borrowing from Catullus, he says of man, "*Odi et amo!* 'Loving thee I hate.' " The poem "Maldrove" then proceeds to question whether he should simplify his paradoxical position and make it the negative discernment of man as "all-abominable." But he decides for the sake of the

few "flowers of beauty"—Achilles or Shelley—upon a ten-
tatively optimistic position:

> I call you all-adorable, O men,
> For the Gods' sakes you might be!

Later the characteristic phrasing tended toward the "all-
abominable," but his attitude has, I think, retained the
early ambivalence. His expressed "hatred" derives from
and is inseparable from his unexpressed "love" of man.
"*Odi et amo*" is the touchstone to Inhumanism.

The tension of loving and hating during the course of
Jeffers' work took on a guise of withdrawal, yet the tension
of the dual emotion remained intact, for he asked mankind
to withdraw with him, to become "all-adorable," or, as he
phrased it in *Roan Stallion* (1925):

> Humanity is the start of the race; I say
> Humanity is the mold to break away from, the crust to
>   break through, the coal to break into fire,
> The atom to be split.

It is doubtful if Jeffers had any more than a hazy notion as
to what he meant by this homily, but his notion clarified
rapidly. He had already cultivated a Spenglerian thesis that
civilization becomes "introverted," that it loses all sense of
striving toward an objective goal. He was able to compose
this thesis with the lesson of his own past life. Had not he
himself, ten years or so before, succeeded in escaping his
personal form of vagrant subjectivity, his frantic concern
with his emotional problems? And had not he, to his own
satisfaction at least, succeeded in solving these problems in
his marriage, his stone house, and his reverence for Nature?
He thought, one supposes, that it would be well if all man-

kind could repeat his experience. He wanted man to deny himself in order to realize himself. He wanted mankind to duplicate the mood of self-rejection which he had set down in his bizarre little story "Mirrors" in 1913 when he was just beginning to react against his emotionalism and dandyism. "Mirrors" tells about one Adair, who, after a disgraceful intimacy with an actress, Millie Gaspard, discovers that his respectable fiancée, Miss Converse, uses one of Millie's love tricks (patting the loved one's hand and using the term of affection "Baby of Love"). He realizes that he himself must have unconsciously communicated it to his fiancée. He cries, "Do you think I can ever marry a woman who has learned the tricks of Millie Gaspard?" His real objection, however, is his recognition of himself in the gesture. "The worst of it," he thinks, "is that . . . we are all mirrors. . . . Everything is like everything else." At this point Jeffers, camouflaged as the impersonal narrator, comments aside: "So that it came to me to understand why Nero sought to destroy the world—because it looked like himself." He concludes: "There is nothing so terrible as one's own likeness. That is why monkeys seem unclean to us."[2]

The disgust that Jeffers directed inward upon his personal passions he also directed outward upon the folly of mankind, whose monstrous hysteria, the first World War, coincided with his own period of serene objectification, and Jeffers recommended—oh, quite sweepingly—that man turn from himself to Nature, where he would find evidence of God. The idea and its peculiarly hard-hearted phrasing had clarified and set by 1927, when he published *The Women at Point Sur:*

> I say that if the mind centers on humanity
> And is not dulled, but remains powerful enough to feel its
>   own and the others, the mind will go mad.
> It is needful to remember the stone and the ocean, without
>   the hills over the house no endurance,
> Without the domed hills and the night.

The doctrine has not manifested any essential change since 1927, although Jeffers has added density and widened the scope of its application. The doctrine, however, had an immediate effect on Jeffers' literary method. Beginning with *The Women at Point Sur,* he fashioned narratives to illustrate what happens to those who refuse to uncenter their minds from humanity. His masochistic religious intensity and his scientific materialism were pressed into service so as to place man in the most alarming neurotic light. Incest became his particular symbol for man's self-consciousness. It is little wonder that people in Carmel took to referring to Jeffers' stone house as his "incestral tower," or that the gnomic intent of these narratives was seldom understood. The material itself was sensational, and readers, after all, are more likely to be impressed by Moll Flanders' dissolute adventures than by her moral resuscitation. The great wonder is that these narratives come off as well as they do. Yet they rise above vulgarity partly because the natural descriptions possess such somber beauty that a balance of sanity remains, and partly because the pathologic characters at times achieve such intensity that one is constrained to admire insanity itself. More pertinently, however, the narratives manage to acquire some dignity because Jeffers relates the violence of his characters and the failures of mankind to a plan of God. But "pattern" is a better word than "plan," for it is in the interplay of recurrent decay and resurgence that Jeffers observes divinity. A question arises: Why, if even decadence and violence are a manifestation of God, should one harangue against them? Jeffers has an answer, no more satisfactory, one must admit, than the theology which holds that free will and God's foreknowledge are not incompatible. But I shall use an analogy to explain Jeffers' stand. The pattern of growth and decay is as inevitable as the tidal rise and fall of the ocean—this is the broad manifestation of the law, and inescapable—but the idiosyncratic motion of ripples may be left to itself. The ripples may run counter to the broad tidal sweep; they will not affect the ultimate pattern. And so for Jeffers, man may in his own mind transcend the tide even while it surges about him. Like Epictetus or Shelley's Prometheus, he admits that he can be restrained or even tortured, but insists that his mind remains always free. This complex of fatalism and voluntarism is best seen in Jeffers' symbol of the "net" or the "trap."

The net for Jeffers is the symbol which permits man to correspond with all other manifestations of the universe. It is his *multum in parvo*. When he describes the involuntary nervous system (as in *Cawdor* and *Such Counsels You Gave to Me*) in such a way as to suggest that he is describing a solar system in a condition of vast, half-conscious somnolence, he is describing what he conceives as a quiddity common to both organic and inorganic existence. The reticulated nerves of the body, the passions, are the net which man is most aware of:

> When I considered it too closely, when I wore it like an
>   element and smelt it like water,
> Life is become less lovely, the net nearer than the skin, a
>   little troublesome, a little terrible.

To allow oneself to surrender absolutely to the net of the nerves is, however, to lose touch with the corresponding net of stars. This is to love humanity rather than God:

> Love, the mad wine of good and evil, the saint's and mur-
> derer's, the mote in the eye that makes its object
> Shine the sun black; the trap in which it is better to catch
> the inhuman God than the hunter's own image.[3]

One must love the divine fate, Jeffers tells us, before one can transcend the human fate. This is the concept dramatized somewhat ambiguously in *Dear Judas*. Christ, like other saviors, according to Jeffers, is the emblem of man's utopian compulsions, the utmost love for humanity. He is most caught in the trap of human fate and struggles most against it and perhaps ultimately contributes most to the divine tidal pattern. Yet he brings more suffering to himself and humanity, Jeffers thinks, than is needful.

Needful or not, no person may entirely escape, for comprehension of the divine fate is premised on the correspondence between the nugatory human passion and the earnest celestial passion. Christ's mother sings:

> I bid you fishermen mending brown nets
> On the white sand,
> I bid you beware of the net, fishermen.
> You never can see it,
> It flies through the white air and we all are snapped in it.
> No, but look round you.
> You see men walking and they seem to be free,
> But look at the faces, they're caught.

Judas also struggles: ". . . what a net of cruelty / Life gasps in, inextricably involved." Jesus realizes that the net is ultimately God's and He realizes also that it is possible to come to relatively peaceful terms with the greater design, but He cannot relinquish His desire for human power. Of Mary's son, He says: "It meant the net of God's will. A song / That fountains power to the powerful . . ." As for Himself, he chooses the power and the suffering which crucifixion perfects:

> Dear Judas, it is God drives us.
> It is not shameful to be duped by God. I have known his
>   glory in my lifetime, I have *been* his glory, I know
> Beyond illusion the enormous beauty of the torch in which
>   our agonies and all are particles of fire.

With this mystical reconciliation, *Dear Judas* becomes ambiguous, for Jeffers' admiration of Jesus' grand effort clouds his distrust of the effort, and Jesus is deified. Lazarus explains to Mary:

> Your son has done what men are not able to do;
> He has chosen and made his own fate. The Roman Caesar
>   will call your son his master and his God; the floods
> That wash away Caesar and divide the booty, shall worship
>   your son. The unconjectured selvages
> And closed orbits of the ocean ends of the earth shall hear
>   of him.

Although Jeffers admires the Promethean sacrifice in these terms, his personal horror of the suffering remains as his argument against Christ's apotheosis, and his position as an Inhumanist seems triumphant in the characterization of Lazarus, who, when Mary asks him if he is not joyful at the glorification of Jesus, says: "No, Mary, I am out of that net. I would to God that you were out of that net."

However ambiguous *Dear Judas* becomes in the strain between conflicting admirations of the Promethean hero and the Inhumanist, there is some reconciliation in Jeffers' intuition that in the last analysis the struggles of mankind are "beautiful." This idea one may extract painfully from *Dear Judas,* but it is stated lucidly enough in a later poem "The Purse-Seine" (1937), where Jeffers describes fishermen at night, commenting:

> I cannot tell you
> How beautiful the scene is, and a little terrible, then, when the crowded fish
> Know they are caught, and wildly beat from one wall to the other of their closing destiny the phosphorescent
> Water to a pool of flame . . .

And a few lines later:

> Lately I was looking from a night
>   mountain-top
> On a wide city, the colored splendor, galaxies of light: how could I help but recall the seine-net
> Gathering the luminous fish? I cannot tell you how beautiful the city appeared, and a little terrible.
> I thought, We have geared the machines and locked all together into interdependence; we have built the great cities; now
> There is no escape. We have gathered vast populations incapable of free survival, insulated
> From the strong earth, each person in himself helpless, on all dependent. The circle is closed, and the net
> Is being hauled in.

Nevertheless, even as the circle closes, Jeffers offers an escape to the individual, the rare individual presumably. He tells him to find the beauty of life by considering the universe wholly:

A severed hand

Is an ugly thing, and man dissevered from the earth and
    stars and his history ... for contemplation or in fact ...
Often appears atrociously ugly. Integrity is wholeness, the
    greatest beauty is
Organic wholeness, the wholeness of life and things, the
    divine beauty of the universe. Love that, not man
Apart from that, or else you will share man's pitiful con-
    fusions, or drown in despair when his days darken.[4]

Nature, Jeffers suggests, can show the way to the Inhumanist's inner salvation by indicating the mutuality between
man and the universe:

The spirit that flickers and hurts in humanity

humanity
Shines brighter from better lamps; but from all shines.
Look to it: prepare for the long winter: spring is far off.[5]

For God wants, he says, "what man's / Feeling for beauty
wants," and "the human sense / Of beauty is our metaphor
of . . . excellence . . . like dust in a whirlwind, making /
The wild wind visible."[6]

2

It will already have occurred to some that Jeffers' doctrine overlaps with Existentialism as another example of a
philosophy of catastrophe. With any number of Jeffers'
pronouncements one may compare the existential feeling
of man's relative unimportance. But there are irreconcilable
differences. Jeffers could no more subscribe to Kierke-
gaard's, Marcel's, or Jaspers' "Christian" God than he could
to Sartre's absence of belief in God. Still more basically, the
Existentialist (and I am aware that I am generalizing about
a philosophy which presents various facets) wishes to be

neither an Idealist nor pragmatist while Jeffers wishes to be both. The Existentialist believes that what seems real is real, and this belief naturally affects the ideals of conduct. But since Jeffers' Inhumanism strives for objectivity at the expense of subjectivity, the problem of conduct must be resolved in an assumed and objective—therefore traditional —morality.

The problem (and this is a transmutation of an emotional problem into philosophical terms) which most burdens Bruce Ferguson in *Mara* is his worry as to whether "we are animals . . . clever in some ways, / Degenerate in others," and followers of "instinct," or whether "we are something else and ought to do otherwise." The implication is, of course, that we ought not to behave like animals but like something else, something capable of overruling instinct. This can only signify one thing; namely, that *Mara* persists as an argument for the ancient concept of reason.

"Reason" may seem a lost and orphaned prescript in the jungle of Jeffers' violence, primitivism, and romantic figuration. Yet consider the allegory of the old man's killing his alter ego in *The Double Axe*. The alter ego, or "the man of terrors," comes with two robbers to steal from the old man. The singing axe kills the robbers, but the old man wakens in time to restrain it from touching "the man of terrors," who admits that he is the old man's other self. Later, in a boat, the old man bids this treacherous self to "Lean forward" and "settle the log more decently / Under that dead thief's head."

> Then the man of terrors
> Understood fate; and his teeth ceased from rattling, his
> face composed itself: "Sharp," he said, "is your mercy,"

And leaned forward over the loaded boat. The old man
    struck once, and fell
On the sand at the boat's tail and lay there senseless
Until the day's end.
                            His axe shook off the blood
    from its eyes and stood guard for him, and his dog
    Snapper
Licked his dead-seeming face. About sundown the old man
    groaned and came to himself, and said,
"It was not easy. Fortunate, Snapper, are all the beasts of the
    mountain: they live their natures: but man
Is outrageous. No man has ever known himself nor sur-
    passed himself until he has killed
Half of himself." He leaned on the boat stern-strake and
    turned his dead man face upward, and the dead face
Was his own in his youth.

One may pause to savor the evidence that even as late as
1948 Jeffers was still destroying his adolescence, and that
this is the personal basis of his Inhumanism. But one may
also recognize that the episode serves as an apologue of the
sacrifice required by the secular aspects of Inhumanism,
and this is surely to be seen as related to "the life of reason."
It is the passions and perhaps the fear of death that the old
man slays.

Jeffers' life of reason is predicated on the correlative
idea that man has his proper place in the universe and that
if he holds to that place he may achieve a "nobility" to
"match the world's," the nobility that Jeffers thinks each
"tragic poet has believed ... possible."[7] The task of finding
and maintaining a natural equilibrium, however, is not
easy; it requires control of the emotions and resistance to
the temptation to stray too far from the natural, "earthly"

life. To get too far from the earth is to lose the primary reality of a relationship to God. But maintaining this reality permits man to realize that: "There are certain duties / Even for . . . modern man."[8] And it permits him to endure human tragedy:

> It is certain the world cannot be stopped
> nor saved.
> It has changes to accomplish and must creep through
> agonies toward new discovery. It must, and it ought:
> the awful necessity
> Is also the sacrificial duty. Man's world is a tragic music
> and is not played for man's happiness,
> Its discords are not resolved but by other discords.
>
> But for each man
> There is real solution, let him turn from himself and man
> to love God. He is out of the trap then. He will remain
> Part of the music, but will hear it as the player hears it.[9]

Most of Jeffers' work has focused on man's inability to abide by reason, but not the least rewarding of his poetry is that which portrays the potential nobility of life. The decent life is scarcely free from pain, but the pain is married to peace. And the peace derives from an awareness of belonging to a dignified order of things. Jeffers writes thus of fishing boats caught in a sudden fog and trying to maintain "a difficult path between the peril of the sea-fog / And the foam on the shore granite."

> One by one, trailing their leader, six crept by me,
> Out of the vapor and into it,
> The throb of their engines subdued by the fog, patient and
> cautious,
> Coasting all round the peninsula

Back to the buoys in Monterey harbor. A flight of pelicans
Is nothing lovelier to look at;
The flight of the planets is nothing nobler; all the arts lose
    virtue
Against the essential reality
Of creatures going about their business among the equally
Earnest elements of nature.[10]

The concept is a little reminiscent of Hardy, as is Jeffers'
poem about a young wife "beyond the narrows of the
Inner Hebrides," who with her adopted child, a "sickly
babe," transfers from a steamer to a skiff that is to bear
them to the small island where she lives.

           The dark-haired girl climbed down to
    it, with one arm holding
That doubtful slip of life to her breast; a tall young man
    with sea-pale eyes and an older man
Helped her; if a word was spoken I did not hear it. They
    stepped a mast and hoisted a henna-color
Bat's wing of sail.
                  Now, returned home
After so many thousands of miles of road and ocean, all
    the hulls sailed in, the houses visited,
I remember that slender skiff with dark henna sail
Bearing off across the stormy sunset to the distant island
Most clearly; and have rather forgotten the dragging whirl-
    pools of London, the screaming haste of New York.[11]

In these poems one is engaged by how different the
tone is from that of the "bitter" poems. They celebrate a
natural life characterized by perils and sadness but also
by tenacity and purpose. And when one reconsiders the
principle of reason in Inhumanism, one begins to sense that
the whole construct is a thoroughly conventional one. But

let us consider how Jeffers has recently phrased his concept
in prose:

It seems time that our race began to think as an adult does,
rather than like an egocentric baby or insane person. This manner of thought and feeling is neither misanthropic nor pessi-
mist, though two or three people have said so and may again. It
involves no falsehoods, and is a means of maintaining sanity in
slippery times; it has objective truth and human value. It offers
a reasonable detachment as rule of conduct, instead of love, hate
and envy. It neutralizes fanaticism and wild hopes; but it provides magnificence for the religious instinct, and satisfies our
need to admire greatness and rejoice in beauty.[12]

In the assault on "love, hate and envy" and upon "fanaticism and wild hopes" one is drawn quite unexpectedly back
to the eighteenth century. One does not wish to tarry here
very long, but there is illumination in making the journey.
We may consider how Swift's method of preaching his
ideal of reasonable behavior included his devastating attack
on triviality, his delight in magnifying human obscenity.
We may remember that *Gulliver's Travels* concludes with
Lemuel's preferring the company of horses to that of men.
Jeffers' technique of exaggerating the wretched and dis-
gusting antics of people in order to emphasize an aim of
prudent conduct is not without precedent.

A final observation, and I am done with the eighteenth
century. It is odd that Jeffers uses the unrestrained, self-
conscious methods of romanticism to argue what at bottom
is an antiromantic ideal. I do not, however, postulate that
Jeffers' formulation is classical. His ethical fervor assumes
the mien of his poetry—and that is luxuriantly romantic.
But I think it is helpful to recognize that Jeffers' verse con-
fronts us not with a romanticism which has worried itself

into exuberant madness but with a classicism that has succumbed to the romantic imagination.

3

Although I have defined Jeffers' doctrine in terms of its disengaged philosophical meaning, there remains the task of considering it in relation to other motives in his poetry. Until this point it has seemed desirable to keep Jeffers' concern with decadence and primitivism separate, or to relate them only in the sense that his interest in primitivism stems from a repugnance toward decadence. But, in coming to a final evaluation of Inhumanism, that separation may be questioned. For, in considering what Jeffers recommends as the desirable life for modern man—the combination of reason and a proximity to Nature—one detects that Jeffers combines elements which are not ordinarily, and probably not easily, cohesive. He asks modern man to be both primitive and profoundly civilized at the same time. He asks him to denature his primitive instincts with civilized reasoning while he insists that he charge his civilization with primitive sensuousness.

One may find the Madrone Bothwell of *Solstice* Jeffers' definitive symbolization of the primitive power of human history. At the same time, however, that he mentions his faith in her regenerative potential, he assails her nature; rather, he permits her to assail her own nature:

> Oh patience, Oh prudence, to be wise once, dreading the cold
> Fury that comes in a moment and tears
> Before it knows. She remembered how it comes, like the entrance of a devil from the red stars
> Crying to be black and cease.

And when she kills her children she moans:

> I was too senseless-confident
> Until the degradation had you in its hands, I did what a
> senseless
> Caged beast killing her cubs . . . Oh . . . Oh . . . Oh . . . I
> beast
> I did it.

As a "beast" Madrone is not a failure in respect of those primitive qualities which are necessary in Jeffers' view for the renewal of culture. But she is a failure as a modern individual. She lacks "patience," "prudence"—reason.

Madrone lacks the calm virtues. However, one must equally suppose that these virtues need to be alloyed with harder elements. In *The Cretan Woman* (1954), Jeffers' recent adaptation of Euripides' *Hippolytus*, Hippolytus is presented as a reserved, rather kindly young man who prefers the friendship of men to the love of women. He seems as disengaged from the passions as Jeffers could wish. His homosexuality is to be seen as an extroverted disaffection with life in perfect contrast to the introverted and involved lesbianism in *The Women at Point Sur*. Yet it is precisely his disengagement that angers Aphrodite. He is too much the Inhumanist, too wise, too "happy." And, indeed, in the characterization of Hippolytus, Jeffers ponders a new possibility in the long Spenglerian rhythms, the possibility not of man's burning up in hysterical flames, but of burning out in too much wisdom. Aphrodite says at the end of the play:

> In future days men will become so powerful
> That they seem to control the heavens and the earth,
> They seem to understand the stars and all science—

Let them beware. Something is lurking hidden.
There is always a knife in the flowers. There is always a
lion just beyond the firelight.

If, as I think, the doctrine of Inhumanism implies a combination of primitive and civilized virtues, it emerges, probably unconsciously, as Jeffers' questioning of his own fatalism. In supporting the virtue of reason, he seems to be pleading for man to recognize that he has arrived at a state wherein the strifes and crudities of barbarism are outmoded. If this is so, then the state of "finishedness," which Spengler broods over, would appear to have for Jeffers its own kind of serene advantage, and he advises modern man to accept this condition and to live accordingly, giving up national competitiveness and wars. Simultaneously he advises that man remain close to Nature so as to eschew the fatal subjectivism that he associates with civilization, and the fatal impotence embodied in Hippolytus. The concept is, of course, idyllic; and further than that, since Jeffers with Calvinistic austerity does not believe that his advice will be or can be followed, the concept is almost paradoxical. Jeffers obviously knows this when he writes:

You have seen through the trick to the beauty;
If we all saw through it, the trick would hardly entice us
and the earth
Be the poorer by many beautiful agonies.[13]

To direct man toward a moral self by means of the wise, the solemn lessons of Nature: that has been Jeffers' life work. He has chosen to work with acid and a needle-pointed stylus; he has beset his lines with crude, angry ornament, has disguised his message and been willing to squander hundreds of lines in febrile hyperbole in order to

justify the admonitory lines. It has not been his nature to
write in the convention of the humanist any more than it
has been the nature of his times to encourage the convention. Nevertheless, beyond his fatalism, beyond his materialism, the God which Jeffers defines is the God who en-
hances and propagates life, human life:

> Is it not by his high superfluousness we know
> Our God? For to equal a need
> Is natural, animal, mineral: but to fling
> Rainbows over the rain
> And beauty above the moon, and secret rainbows
> On the domes of deep sea-shells,
> And make the necessary embrace of breeding
> Beautiful also as fire,
> Not even the weeds to multiply without blossom
> Nor the birds without music:
> There is the great humaneness at the heart of things,
> The extravagant kindness, the fountain
> Humanity can understand, and would flow likewise
> If power and desire were perch-mates.[14]

No doubt the attacks upon contemporary man have been
overstated, but when Jeffers addresses "the future children"
one rediscovers the tenderer half of *odi et amo:*

>   O future children:
> Cruelty is dirt and ignorance, a muddy peasant
> Beating his horse. Ambition and power-lust
> Are for adolescents and defective persons. Moderate kind-
>   ness
> Is oil on a crying wheel: use it. Mutual help
> Is necessary: use it when it is necessary.
> And as to love: make love when need drives.
> And as to love: love God.[15]

The question which Jeffers has asked is: If there is beauty of the world and potential beauty in mankind, and if there exists a "great humaneness at the heart of things," why has man failed to be beautiful and humane? He thinks he knows why, and his doctrine of Inhumanism seeks to guide us from the pitfalls. It is the critical absurdity of the century to insist that this doctrine has anything in common with nihilism. Inhumanism asks that man achieve serenity and security by retaining the terrestrial wisdom of Silenus even as he graduates from the modern university: to be both primitive and civilized. Primitive and civilized, and in the best senses of these words.

VIII

The Creed of Permanence

1

IF WE ASSUME a principle that mood and style are con-
terminous, we assume that a given mind will re-create
itself in forms corresponding in some recognizable way to
the primary yearnings of the temperament. If we hold the
principle to this expression it remains valuable, but if we
shift terms, we may run into nonsense. We may infer, for
example, that a "bad" style reflects a "bad" concept, while,
as a matter of fact, it may only indicate that a writer is
technically incapable of communicating. We may not, I
think, entertain the notion that goodness or badness of
style derives from the ethical position of the artist. I do not,
however, deny that one temperament will produce a tendency toward a formulation different from that of another
temperament.

Like the terms in trigonometry, the relationship between personality and form is the expression of an abstrac-
tion. It is imperative to understand and appreciate the
dynamics of the relationship—that in itself is not responsible for taste and skill, which ultimately determine style—

before attempting to evaluate how competently the creator deploys his reason, learning, and self-disciplines.

Robinson Jeffers' temperament consolidates in a mood of tragic acquiescence, but two quarreling compulsions underlie: a compulsion toward the denouements of "prophetic doom" and a compulsion toward the resurgence of titanic discovery. As the oracular prophet, Jeffers accepts and embraces an isolation which permits him to disregard his social environment in general and his audience in particular. He reminds Cassandra that her apocalyptic utterance cannot be popular. Perhaps she should tell lies, be optimistic and be "praised for kindly / Wisdom"?

> No: you'll still mumble in a corner a crust of truth, to men
> And gods disgusting.—You and I, Cassandra.[1]

When the human mind presupposes that what it has to say will be disregarded, it will cease in large measure to attempt to please an audience, although it will not cease to try to please itself. The very isolation may, indeed, be a source of aristocratic pleasure: "To be truth-bound, the neutral / Detested by all the dreaming factions, is my errand here."[2] This dour and proud insularity of the prophetic enunciation may, and usually does, permit a poet to justify a looseness in his verse structure. He will not honey his lines who thinks no one will read them—he may abandon all device for what he sees as his superiority, his solace, his revenge, that is, his "truth," which does not change simply because no one pays attention. We may observe some such development in the difference between Blake's earlier poetry and his rambling prophetic books. We may observe a movement toward relaxation of form between *Californians* and the later, sprawling narratives.

And what of the other compulsion, the urge toward self-assertion, titanic climax? Here, too, one may anticipate reflection in form, probable co-ordinates, like the linked characteristics which biologists tell us repose in the germ cell. One may expect a tendency toward intensification of emotion and hyperbole of language. In essence the Promethean drive signifies a desire for rebirth, intuitively recognizing the elements of violence, catastrophe, and terror which accompany such a labor. These elements emerge in language and situation. We feel their vital motion through Shelley's hyperboles, Melville's superb, although often wrenched, metaphors.

The apocalyptic and titanic monopolies of Jeffers' personality have imposed corresponding symbols on the poetry. The prophet of doom takes delight in the ravage of destructive fire and, more particularly, in the immensity of night wherein, one by one, the fires of the stars are burning out. The rejection of doom evoked by the Promethean nature rises in the recurring symbol of the hawk, the fierce, uncompromising, ascending bird whose will is simply the will to live. But if these two compulsions oppose each other, they are concordant at one point: they equally permit a proud disdain. And so (I assume) when critical revulsion toward *The Women at Point Sur* arose, Jeffers could take solace both in a prophetic and a Titanic isolation. He could write of "The Bird with the Dark Plumes":

> The bird with the dark plumes in my blood,
> That never for one moment, however I patched my truces,
> Consented to make peace with the people,
> It is pitiful now to watch her pleasure in a breath of tempest
> Breaking the sad promise of spring. . . .

Poor outlaw that would not value their praise do you prize
  their blame?
"Their liking," she said, "was a long creance,
But let them be kind enough to hate me, that opens the
  sky."
It is almost as foolish my poor falcon
To want hatred as to want love; and harder to win.

Hand in hand with the encouragement toward structural relaxation that a temperamental isolation gives go other more exterior forces which tend toward looseness.

Those who object to Jeffers' technique insist that his clambering lines result from an inability to achieve anything else. No doubt he has come to be pretty much committed to an informality. One should, however, remember that as a young man Jeffers achieved a certain metrical virtuosity. *Californians* contains examples of *terza rima,* Spenserian stanzas, and very regular iambic pentameter. And if some of his later conventional efforts are as uncomfortable as farm hands dressed in their Sunday best, there are also some fine sonnets and, upon rare occasions, a beautiful variation of the ballad form:

"Why do you never lie
On my breast, my dear love?"
"Oh, that was another sky.
Here, each of us on his own,
Each on his own back-bone,
My dear love."

"Is that the law of this land,
Each one of us on his own?"
"Oh, yes, we are underground
With the elves and fairies: lonely

Is the word in this country,
My dear love."

"What, a law in this land
That breast can never meet breast?"
'After while you will understand.
The mole is our moon, and worms
Are the stars we observe,
My dear love."[3]

At this point the conclusion I wish to draw is that Jeffers has not assumed a laxity in his mature work solely because of an inability to conform to the demands of regular meter and rhyme, but that as his artistic temperament set in the mold, precision of form became alien to much that he wished to say. We may observe the transition between the traditional prosody of *Californians* and the unconventional prosody of the later work in the poem *The Coast-Range Christ,* written before *Tamar* but not published until 1925. *The Coast-Range Christ,* a poem of over five hundred lines, is written in rhymed couplets, and the metrical pattern observes in general a seven-stress line. The composition of the feet, however, is capricious, and it is in the emphasis of a prosody based on stress rather than on regular feet, and in the long line, that the nature of the transition lies. Jeffers attained his eventual meter, that long, ritualistic line, by the process of dropping the rhyme used in *The Coast-Range Christ* and altering the number of stresses in his basic line from seven to five or ten.

There are lapses, to be sure, where no pattern seems to exist. When these occur at transitional points, such as shifting from one setting to another in the longer poems, I think the reader will find them, at worst, unimportant.

But sometimes the lapses are unfortunate, for they leave the poetry embarrassingly suspended between passages of stridulous prose. This is to speak of Jeffers' metrical technique at its worst. To consider it at its best is to recognize that the heavy, sullen rhythm is a dimension of the dark, humorless tales.

2

Although Jeffers received a good foundation in classical languages as a youth, it would appear that in later life he mainly consulted translations of Greek and Latin literature. His enthusiasm, however, for the classics reveals itself not only in his adaptations of Greek themes but also in some of the elements of his style. In the middle work from *Cawdor* to *Such Counsels You Gave to Me* he experimented with a few of the devices which are the stock of classical epic: apostrophe, heroic simile, and a deliberately anacoluthic flexibility of syntax which encourages the impression that the poet is simultaneously involved in, and analytical of, a situation, or that a situation possesses a past value that is coeval with a present one. This delicate blurring of temporal reality, this intimation of separate yet coexistent worlds develops from time to time in Vergil's descriptions of action. One finds it occasionally in the slight grammatical shifts (italicized below) of Jeffers' lines:

> If I were hunting in the Ventana canyons again with my
>   strong sons, *and to sleep under stars,*
> I should be happy again.[4]

This one device, which draws nourishment from parallel emotional and intellectual positions, realizes an inevitability, a perfection. But one suspects that most of Jeffers' classical mannerisms are accretions. They display his admiration for traditional artistry, but they do not always seem to belong in the verse. The least happy examples occur in the volumes between *The Women at Point Sur* (1927) and *Be Angry at the Sun* (1941), the period when Jeffers appears to have striven to capture the high seriousness of traditional tragedy.

During the same period, the language sometimes assumes an "Elizabethan" quality. I do not wish to burden with examples where the judgment remains subjective, but perhaps one line from *Cawdor* will serve to illustrate my impression: "If you were full of eyes you'd find no fault in him." This, to me, is not unlike some of Edwin Arlington Robinson's lines, and, like them, reflects a conscious appreciation of the linguistic bravado of the Renaissance. Without recalling any particular dramatist, it reminds me of the half-brash, half-miraculous conceits of the later Stuart drama.

In addition to classical and Renaissance tendencies, one finds in the considerable alliteration an awareness of the formalities of old Germanic verse. One can point to examples that offend by their heaviness, but Jeffers has often used alliteration with remarkable flair. Sometimes a "divided" alliteration brings to mind the Anglo-Saxon device of reinforcing stress with alliteration:

> O blossom of fire, bitter to men,
> Watchdog of the woeful days,
> How many sleepers
> Bathing in peace, dreaming themselves delight,
> All over the city, all over the Argolid plain, all over the
>   dark earth,
> (Not me, a deeper draught of peace

And darker waters alone may wash me)
Do you, terrible star, star without pity,
Wolf of the east, waken to misery.[5]

The skill is found in the willingness to abandon the pattern or to alter it, to soften the echo by alliterating an unstressed syllable (delight) or by substituting for alliteration the repetition of words or phrases (in the fifth and eighth lines, "all over" and "star"); and yet in spite of variations to preserve a continuity—here, the gay flash of the shuttle which is weaving the sad cloth of doom.

3

As the natural directions of Jeffers' temperament stretch toward an informal prosody, so also his conception of the relationship of poetry to prose contributes toward the same end. In the twentieth century the prestige of fiction has tended to induce among poets a desire to stress the separate character of poetry by removing it as far as possible from prose. This has led to experimentation, sometimes rewarding, sometimes empty. But Jeffers wanted not to experiment but to "reclaim some of the power and reality" which he thought poetry "was so hastily surrendering to prose."

The modern French poetry . . . and the most "modern" of the English poetry, seemed to me thoroughly defeatist, as if poetry were in terror of prose, and desperately trying to save its soul from the victor by giving up its body. It was becoming slight and fantastic, abstract, unreal, eccentric; and was not even saving its soul, for these are generally anti-poetic qualities. It must reclaim substance and sense, and physical and psychological reality. This feeling has been basic in my mind since then. It led me to write narrative poetry, and to draw subjects from contemporary life; to present aspects of life that modern poetry had generally avoided; and to attempt the expression of philosophic and scientific ideas in verse. It was . . . in my mind . . . only to reclaim old freedom.[6]

Jeffers' choice of form, then, was in part determined by a decision to risk meeting prose on its own grounds. That meant loosening the reins. But how far could his verse go toward prose without becoming prose—or what is more likely, bad prose? No doubt he permitted his blank verse to relax dangerously but, to counterbalance the looseness, he adopted a lavish, heightened rhetoric.

The power of Jeffers' language depends partly upon the immediacy of his direct description but in greater measure upon his faith in images. Like the Anglo-Saxon poets, with whom he shares this faith, Jeffers has produced some of the best metaphors and some of the worst. The worst derive from his wish to describe people in terms of vast geographies or to describe impersonal objects in animate terms. When Madrone Bothwell "kills" her former husband's automobile, Jeffers employs a figure that would have brought deep sorrow to Ruskin: "The gas-line dripped stinking blood and the car died." The incongruity needs no comment. His best images reflect his desire to freeze to a standstill the running beauty of natural things; they are embedded sparingly in the matrix of simple language. The phrasing and concept of the sonnet "Return," for example, achieve an inevitability, as though Yeats had traded his falcons for California hawks, and his beloved moths for May-flies:

> A little too abstract, a little too wise,
> It is time for us to kiss the earth again,

It is time to let the leaves rain from the skies,
Let the rich life run to the roots again.
I will go down to the lovely Sur Rivers
And dip my arms in them up to the shoulders.
I will find my accounting where the alder leaf quivers
In the ocean wind over the river boulders.
I will touch things and things and no more thoughts,
That breed like mouthless May-flies darkening the sky,
The insect clouds that blind our passionate hawks
So that they cannot strike, hardly can fly.
Things are the hawk's food and noble is the mountain, Oh
    noble
Pico Blanco, steep sea-wave of marble.

The mention of Yeats summons up the poems of Jeffers' journey through Ireland and England in 1929. Collected under the title *Descent to the Dead* (1931), they may well represent his highest performance in the medium of short poems. The somber metrical patterns develop so inexorably that one tends to ascribe a strict regularity to them. And the language ascends slowly until the poems emerge harsh yet glowing, all their resonances intact. "Shakespeare's Grave" from the collection is to my mind a permanency:

"Doggerel," he thought, "will do for churchwardens,
Poetry's precious enough not to be wasted,"
And rhymed it all out with a skew smile:
"Spare these stones. Curst be he that moves my bones—
Will hold the hands of masons and grave-diggers."
But why did the good man care? For he wanted quietness.
He had tasted enough life in his time
To stuff a thousand; he wanted not to swim wide
In waters, nor wander the enormous air,
Nor grow into grass, enter through the mouths of cattle

The bodies of lusty women and warriors,
But all be finished. He knew it feelingly; the game
Of the whirling circles had become tiresome.
"Annihilation's impossible, but insulated
In the church under the rhyming flagstone
Perhaps my passionate ruins may be kept off market
To the end of this age. Oh, a thousand years
Will hardly leach," he thought, "this dust of that fire."

The power to command compelling imagery often diminishes as a poet comes into middle age. A diminution of imagery, rather than of concept, for example, characterizes Wordsworth's later periods. Jeffers' sense of metaphor, however, has remained acute, and I think the century will not produce more forceful imagery than that which occurs in his most recent poetry. One example:

There is another nature of fire, but the same fire,
Slayer of forests: lion-color bulks of flame burst through the
    trunks
And the trees crash, flame runs like monkeys among the
    branches...[7]

The audacity and barbaric clash of such tropes will perhaps offend the sensibilities of a mind attracted to the calm virtues of balance and elegance.

Reviewing the *Medea* for *The Kenyon Review,* Dudley Fitts notes the structural improvements that Jeffers makes in the play and then quotes the following lines:

I will look at the light of the sun, this last time. I wish from
    that blue sky the white wolf of lightning
Would leap, and burst my skull and my brain and like a
    burning babe cling to these breasts ...
[SHE CHECKS AND LOOKS FIERCELY AT THE WOMEN BELOW.]

Mr. Fitts comments:

Well might she check at such a metaphor: it would have floored
the Ancient Pistol himself. But it is not merely that the language is comically forced. What is significant is the unheard but
remembered counterpoint of Euripides's heroine chanting at
this same point—wildly, indeed, but with a control of phrasing
and image that makes this acrobatic white wolf silly enough.
The Euripidean energy—and he was not a moderate man—has
been transformed into as coarse a ranting as ever fluttered the
nickelodeons.[8]

Mr. Fitts, in collaboration with Robert Fitzgerald, has
obliged the contemporary reader with careful and proper
renditions of Sophocles. He has shown one way, but not
the only way, that Hellenic art can be successfully tendered
to the modern audience. His objection to Jeffers' language
is understandable as the reflection of a legitimate literary
bias. The offending metaphor is certainly not Jeffers' hap-
piest; nevertheless, in its very shiftings it circumscribes with
imaginative force what might transpire in electrocution.
But the essential justification for the metaphor is to be
found in the play itself; it lies in the elucidation of the
conflict in Medea between the "white wolf" of her vengeful,
primitive nature and the "burning babe" of her equally
primitive maternalism. Of course, however, if one reads a
play while listening to the "remembered counterpoint" of
someone else, he may very well miss even the most basic
position of that play.

4

Although Jeffers' technique is founded on certain accidents of his environment and training and, in larger measure, on the internecine strife of his personality, to arrive

at a full appreciation of Jeffers' style, it is necessary to educe his faith in "permanency." This faith relates to the primitivism in his philosophic Inhumanism; in his poetry it is expressed in the repeated symbol of stone. And it comes to the surface as a formal literary creed:

Fashions, forms of machinery, the more complex social, financial, political adjustments, and so forth, are all ephemeral, exceptional; they exist but will never exist again. Poetry must concern itself with (relatively) permanent things. These have poetic value; the ephemeral has only news value.[9]

I think that this signifies that Jeffers elected to write in the pastoral tradition. If his characters are not purely primitive, they nevertheless inhabit a scene which is purely natural. A pastoral enthusiasm runs counter to most of the significant achievements in modern poetry, yet it avoids one of the subterfuges of the modern verse which pretends to urbanity, the subterfuge of contending that the urbane consciousness is best expressed not in the wry, realistic terms of Juvenal or Dr. Johnson but in the haunting tones of *Alastor*. But is not the dilemma of the mood patent? *The Waste Land,* for example, grafts the pastoral tradition upon the city scene. I assume that the precedent for city poetry in Eliot's case is French symbolism. However true this may be, the effect of *The Waste Land* is not so much that of French symbolism as it is that of James Thomson's *The City of Dreadful Night* (1874). When this connection is observed, one sees that *The Waste Land* describes the bifurcation of a consciousness which, like Shelley's, desires to flee from Coke Town but, unlike Shelley's, deliberately restrains itself. At the same time, this consciousness compensates for the restraint by transforming the city by means of a gothic-pastoral idiom and by divorcing man from the generalized swarm (regarded by the Juvenalian mind) and transforming him into a lonely pastoral hero: a ship-wrecked shepherd, disguised or bewitched, wandering about a queer, hostile island. The dilemma of this mood— one can scarcely call it a "conception"—is reflected in Eliot's title, *The Waste Land,* a pastoral description of an urbane condition. The same dilemma is reflected in many oxymoronic titles such as Parker Tyler's *The Granite Butterfly* (1945) and John F. Nims' *The Iron Pastoral* (1947). What these titles suggest is that the poets wish to borrow earnestness from the eternal forms of Nature. This is an aim which Jeffers has pursued with greater openness.

Jeffers' insistence on the "relatively permanent things" has separated him in other ways from the main currents of contemporary poetry. In setting up his idea of what the great poet should accomplish in our time (and the portrait, quite understandably, turns out to be of himself), he writes:

What seems to me certain is that this hypothetical great poet would break sharply away from the directions that are fashionable in contemporary poetic literature. He would understand that Rimbaud was a young man of startling genius, but not to be imitated; and that "The Waste Land," though one of the finest poems of this century and surely the most influential, marks the close of a literary dynasty, not the beginning. He would think of Gerard Hopkins as a talented eccentric, whose verse is so overloaded with self-conscious ornament and improbable emotion that it is hardly readable, except by enthusiasts, and certainly not a model to found one's work on, but a shrill note of warning.

Aside from these instances, and to put the matter more fundamentally, I believe that our man would turn away from the self-consciousness and naive learnedness, the undergraduate irony, unnatural metaphors, hiatuses and labored obscurity that are too prevalent in contemporary verse. His poetry would be natural and direct. He would have something new and important to say, and just for that reason he would wish to say it clearly. He would be seeking to express the spirit of his time (as well as all times), but it is not necessary, because an epoch is confused, that its poet should share its confusions.[10]

There is nothing new in the concept. Yvor Winters, for example, shares the opinion, although his idea of its application is thoroughly different. But whether one agrees with Winters' or Jeffers' ideal of poetic expression, the principle, which essentially longs for clarity and objectivity, indicates a way, perhaps the only way, for poetry to persist as a force in a predominantly prosaic culture.

Jeffers' poetic equipage will be argued among the classrooms of the future. Always in primarily timid eras, like our own, it will be censured, as Whitman's "barbaric yawp" most often is today. Yet I believe that even today, despite the clutter of taut and slack strands, the horrendous inconsistencies, we may value the greatness of a voice which exceeds mere idiom. In a fit of impatience one may wish he had blotted a thousand lines, but the wish is unrealistic. In Jeffers' poetry we gather the prodigality of Nature, teeming not solely with blossom and fruit, but also with weed and thorn, for Jeffers' earth is the complete earth, the "daedal earth" that Lucretius and Spenser mention with reverence.

And even today we ought to discover that the key to Jeffers' esthetics is not to be found among the nods and minuets of diction but in the postures of concept. But then, it is always strength of concept, never worship of superficial form, that brings a poet to ripeness and to greatness. (I must, I suppose, iterate here that I am not concerned with any ethical position in relation to "style," but with a militant thinking which might adventitiously include an ethical position.) America has produced three great poets in the century which has seen her rise to greatness—Eliot, Frost, and Jeffers. And each of these first and foremost is a thinking man, responding to the same central question of his age: What is the destiny of man? And each has responded differently. Eliot represents one extreme of response in asking for rebirth through Christianity; Jeffers represents an opposite extreme in asking for a rationalism based ultimately on a scientifically objective view of life; Frost has struck a bitter-sweet balance, believing that somehow the quality of good will triumph over the quantity of bad. And each of these has developed a voice consonant with his thought: Eliot's literary language condescending continuously to the colloquial; Jeffers' colloquial language stretching continuously toward the literary; and Frost, once more balanced, restraining his idiom so as to avoid either the literary or the colloquial. But Eliot's and Frost's concepts have been well understood. Not so with Jeffers. Indeed, those very critics who have accused him of a want of subtlety have consistently demonstrated his greatest subtlety by mistaking his premises for his conclusions. Yet the proper conclusions—not frightening, not morbid, not deranged—are always easily accessible for the reader whose imagination has survived Brooks and Warren, and who sympathetically realizes that thought can be held with such intensity that it becomes in itself form and content and in so doing becomes emotion.

IX

The Debate

1

THE CREATIVE IMAGINATION is a selective instrumentality that rearranges the experience which whirls about one with the accidental and baffling insistence of a blizzard. Even more, the mature imagination qualifies the experience to some extent, arranging the response even before the experience occurs. The poet in this way is the slave of the genii he has let out of the bottle. His vision becomes relatively inflexible, and externals tend to blend into the patterns which this vision imposes. Sometimes, though rarely, circumstances assemble to alter the vision. Oftener, once the focus is set, it stands; the poet may gain power or grow in technical skill, but he will continue to see his world in an unalterable way. This at once constitutes his strengths and weaknesses.

By the time he had written *The Women at Point Sur* (1927), Robinson Jeffers had consolidated his experience and he ceased to receive any essentially new insights; what was factually new he tended to file away with what was

imaginatively established. For better or worse he had
forged a fictive attitude which, though it was in part the
result of experience, has since tyrannized his subsequent
experience. The attitude, by no means simple, may be described in a general way as a simultaneously sardonic and
elegiac melancholy. This mood in the narratives may make
Jeffers seem "bitter" rather than sad, yet I think the central
nature of his feeling is as I have described it. There are
limitations to the mood, and Jeffers seems to be aware of
them:

When I think, I know that pleasure and pain counterbalance
each other pretty accurately on the average, but when I write
verses I am just the opposite apparently of that delightful fellow Ford Madox Ford writes about, who "had tried so hard to
be a philosopher, but cheerfulness *would* come creeping in."
However, our ends tend to be rather sad, and we bawl at birth;
I suppose my verses are thinking of the ends of life, and with
what sort of hard faces to meet them, rather than the way-
stations . . .[1]

It seems evident that the restrictions of Jeffers' elegiac
mood are too severe to foster a broad understanding of
character such as narrative or dramatic poetry requires.
And this indeed is the primary restriction upon Jeffers'
ability as a storyteller. Because he himself tends to see
things in a light of resigned sadness, he thinks also that
this is the way his characters ought to come to see them.
One can put up with a single Hamlet in a play—three or
four are troublesome. Furthermore, it is questionable
whether in any final sense the character committed to his
own tragedy can achieve tragedy, for he is on the one hand
too aware of his own condition and on the other hand too
little aware of the condition of others to oppose the circum-

stances of fate or accident with any show of confidence. There is a greater difficulty: Jeffers' omnipresent doctrine of Inhumanism which, as an injunction to avoid those very passions which underlie tragedy, is hostile to spontaneity in character. It is true that of all his "tragic" characters only Orestes and Lazarus are absolutely Inhumanists; nevertheless, the doctrine itself haunts the narratives; if the characters do not assail their own "human" natures, Jeffers by interpolation does it for them.

Despite these fundamental limitations, Jeffers has tried with solemnity and energy to be a tragic poet. His sights have been fixed on "our ends" which "tend to be rather sad," and he has occupied himself with the counterpoint of rise and fall, which he says "God and the tragic poets . . . love."[2] The pattern has remained fairly constant, but his theory of what tragedy should accomplish appears to have changed. Early in his career (ca. 1925) in a manuscript note written for his own instruction, he scribbled that a story that "attains significant release":

. . . will influence its reader in the same sense, and this is good for him, it is moral. It is a "happy ending," for something happens, whether marriage or escape or sudden death, a lysis, a freeing of some sort; and a settlement, an adjusted balance.[3]

From this note it would appear that Jeffers' early aim in his narratives was an Aristotelian catharsis and that the intent was, if not instructional, "moral." His later concept of tragedy, however, as stated in 1948, has denied the moralistic principle:

Tragedy has been regarded, ever since Aristotle, as a moral agent, a purifier of the mind and emotions. But the story of Medea is about a criminal adventurer and his gun-moll; it is no more moral than the story of Frankie and Johnny; only more ferocious. And so with the yet higher summits of Greek tragedy, the Agamemnon series and the Oedipus Rex; they all tell primitive horror-stories, and the conventional pious sentiments of the chorus are more than balanced by the bad temper and wickedness, or folly, of the principal characters. What makes them noble is the poetry; the poetry, and the beautiful shapes of the plays, and the extreme violence born of extreme passion.[4]

I do not know how seriously we are expected to take this half-truth as an analysis of Greek drama. I do know that we are not obliged to acquiesce in an author's self-analysis when it is not borne out by that author's accomplishment. The statement might apply to his adaptations of Euripides' plays. It will hardly apply to the narratives, which have become increasingly moralistic over the years—so much so that they have tended to dissociate themselves from tragedy altogether.

2

I have previously suggested that the narratives contain stylistic elements which appear to derive from Stuart drama. There is another and more radical way in which the narratives echo the tones of the Renaissance, and this is Jeffers' apparent effort to commingle the modern concept of the unconscious with the Elizabethan concept of "monomania." King Lear comes to mind as a conspicuous example of the motive. Temporarily maddened by the unfilial behavior of his elder daughters, he accounts for the grief of others on the basis of his own. Hence, when he finds Edgar lamenting his devils, he thinks that Edgar's "daughters" have "brought him to this pass." In *Give Your Heart to the Hawks,* Lance Fraser's mental anguish springs not solely from his having murdered his brother but also from the conflict between his desire for punishment and his wife's advice to forget his guilt and avoid punishment. When he encounters some stray cattle on the narrow trail along which he and Fera are fleeing from the scene of his crime, his "ruling passion" dictates that the cattle are punishers:

> Albeit a part of his mind was awake and faintly
> Knew what they were; the master part willed them to be
> Men pursuing a murderer . . .

The motive continues into later work. In *Mara* Bruce Ferguson, unable to face the fact of his wife's infidelity and the cloud of impurity that surrounds him, yearns for a "huge / Blade and tumor of a wave to come and wash clean." Later the longing becomes a violent fantasy. Drinking in a bar in the company of prostitutes, he thinks of "enormous antlers" emerging from the sea and annihilating the world. The dream of purification by the sea finally controls him:

> He looked at the woman's
> Trivial fat face; she sidled closer to him and said,
> "I'm thirsty, dear." He said, "That's the salt sea.
> I never slept with a drowned woman: what d'y' charge
> On the sea-weed bed under the little swimming fishes?"

Jeffers' sometimes clumsy, sometimes felicitous acknowledgment of Renaissance drama and his efforts to rework Greek drama suggest that in his own mind he wished to acknowledge both traditions by blending the Greek conception of an abstract fate with the Renaissance conception of a psychological fate. Either of these is potentially rich in dramatic situations, but together they are burdensome. One wonders how much "fate" human nature can tolerate. The deck is emphatically stacked against his characters, and, in being so exorbitant, the determinism gravely weakens dramatic possibilities. When to this inordinate determinism is added Jeffers' doctrine of Inhumanism, the dramatic possibilities at the level of character all but vanish. This is a matter on which Yvor Winters has written with considerable eloquence.

Like most critics, Mr. Winters assumes that Jeffers' philosophy is tantamount to nihilism:

> Life as such is incest, an insidious and destructive evil. So much, says Mr. Jeffers by implication, for Greek and Christian ethics. Now the mysticism of such a man as San Juan de la Cruz offers at least the semblance of a spiritual, a human, discipline as a preliminary to union with Divinity; but for Mr. Jeffers a simple and mechanical device lies always ready; namely, suicide, a device to which he has, I believe, never resorted.

I have already endeavored in previous chapters to indicate that Jeffers' aim—preached by direct statement as well as by dramatic example—is conventional morality, endurance, discipline, and the avoidance of violence. I shall not argue these conclusions further. But if I am correct, then Mr. Winters is not, and his misunderstanding of Inhumanism leads him to misinterpretations of the narratives. Of *The Women at Point Sur* he writes:

> *The Women at Point Sur* is a perfect laboratory of Mr. Jeffers' philosophy and a perfect example of his narrative method. Barclay, an insane divine, preaches Mr. Jeffers' religion, and his disciples, acting upon it, become emotional mechanisms, lewd and twitching conglomerations of plexuses, their humanity annulled. Human experience in these circumstances, having necessarily and according to the doctrine, no meaning,

there can be no necessary sequence of events: every act is equiva-
lent to every other; every act is devoid of consequence and occurs in a perfect vacuum; most of the incidents could be shuffled
about into different sequences without violating anything save
Mr. Jeffers' sense of their relative intensity.

I wish to share Mr. Winters' reservations about *The
Women at Point Sur* as a work of art, but not his confusions
about it as doctrine. Barclay, as I have already taken pains
to demonstrate, does not preach Jeffers' "religion," but the
opposite of his religion. Nor do Barclay's "disciples" (if by
"disciples" Mr. Winters means the other main characters in
the narrative) act upon it. They are, as a matter of fact,
only faintly aware of what Barclay is up to and they go
pretty much their own ways. They are indeed "lewd and
twitching" (it is impossible to improve on Mr. Winters'
diction when he is inspired by indignation), but they are
connected with Jeffers' creed only by a relationship of
antipathy. However, on the basis of what he considers Jeffers' beliefs, Mr. Winters concludes that Jeffers:

... has abandoned narrative logic with the theory of ethics, and
he has never, in addition, achieved a distinguished style: his
writing, line by line, is pretentious trash. There are a few good
phrases, but they are very few, and none is first-rate.[5]

Jeffers ignored the attack, and although many came to
his defense, perhaps the most pertinent comments belong
to those with whom Mr. Winters presumably had much in
common. Noting Winters' deduction that Jeffers' "characters are incapacitated from having free will and acting
morally" as a result of Jeffers' believing in a "mechanism-
God," John Crowe Ransom smilingly suggested that the
argument "may be too ingenious, like an argument that is

merely academic; for Jeffers' characters may have the illusion of moral freedom . . . or his readers may have it; in which case it might require a whole plot to bring about the final refutation, and the total effect would be a large single one, like that of tragedy."[6] Presumably Mr. Ransom was more interested in chastising Mr. Winters than in defending Robinson Jeffers.

Allen Tate, the most hospitable and in many ways the most sensitive of the "new critics," remarked:

[Jeffers] has been attacked by Yvor Winters as a decadent romantic and there is some truth in the charge because Jeffers' long narrative poems deal with murder, incest, and other violent actions. But he is—in "Roan Stallion," "The Women at Point Sur," and "Tamar"—a poet of great power; and his short poems—they can scarcely be called lyrics—achieve a fine restraint and modulation of tone.[7]

Although I cannot subscribe to Mr. Winters' estimate, I am more than willing to extract from his critique a very useful insight. Mr. Winters suggests that since the long poems fail as logical narrative, they could perhaps be regarded as extraordinarily long lyrics. Here, too, he concludes (quite rightly) that they fail.[8] Yet Mr. Winters is singularly guilty of a "black-or-white" fallacy when he suggests that the only alternative to narrative or dramatic poetry is the lyric. Another possibility comes to mind, the general outlines of which Amos Wilder has already prescribed by referring to the long poems as "hymns of salvation."[9]

3

Among the "reasonable raptures" of Jeffers' early reading were the plays of Christopher Marlowe. In a short poem

"That Noble Flower" (1941) he paid homage to Marlowe in such a way as to suggest that he felt some kinship with him:

> Oh, noble, rich, glowing color of blood,
> Too strong for the modern world to admire:
> But Shakespeare's and Marlowe's audiences
> Heard your hot red trumpet-call
> At every turning of the steep tragedy;
> And at the end: the stage
> Heaped with corpses and a few solemn words.

Jeffers has paid even more telltale homage. In *Give Your Heart to the Hawks* Lance Fraser goes to the grave of his brother and prays, "What must I do? . . . I cannot live as I am." He is seeking sanity and salvation, yet he knows that it is too late for him to hope for these things. Momentarily, however, he thinks that his brother appears and forgives him. When the hallucination passes, Lance says, "It has all been useless and blind. I am back in hell." Then his father cries:

> If you had listened in the days before: now it is night,
> And who shall hear? but the sharp feet of pursuers: yet
>   look how Christ's blood
> Flows like a fiery comet through heaven and would rain
>   sweetness
> The fields refuse.

One recognizes, quite suddenly, when one encounters the words, "look how Christ's blood / Flows like a fiery comet through heaven," that Jeffers, whether consciously or unconsciously, is reworking the final scene of *Doctor Faustus*. Oscillating between heaven and hell, Faustus also thinks of salvation too late.

See, see where Christ's blood streams in the firmament.
One drop would save my soul, half a drop, ah, my Christ.

Marlowe's vision was primarily naturalistic. He was inclined to see the deteriorated man and a sad landscape, ruined and distant from Eden. Whatever loftiness he attained in drama, he attained not by vaulting over the debris of life, which he saw everywhere about him, but by crawling over it. We observe this in particular in his first play *Tamburlaine,* wherein there is little to choose between Christian and barbarian. The same scorn appears in *The Jew of Malta,* where it is difficult to condone the behavior of either Barabas or his Christian judges; and when Barabas is caught in his own trap, one feels neither irony nor justice but relief that the savage farce is ended. The relief, however, is sustaining, for the details, accumulating less realistically than oppressively, finally demand a neutralization of evil. And this is the pattern of Marlowe's drama; the evil cancels itself, revenge falls equally upon the unjust and the unjust. The effect is magnificent, but I think one may reasonably doubt that Marlowe wrote tragedy. Perhaps *Edward the Second* approaches it, yet here, as with *Dido, Queen of Carthage,* the sequence of events was fairly well restricted by preconceptions of historical "fact." He does not mutilate this fact although he somewhat changes it.

Among the basic reasons that Marlowe did not and could not write the kind of tragedy which Shakespeare, for example, wrote, was that whereas Shakespeare was *aware* of the split between Renaissance naturalism and the medieval faith in human destiny, Marlowe was *obsessed* by it. His obsession induced him to exaggerate the dis-

crepancy by emphasizing naturalistic detail and sordid
motives. We are made particularly aware of the naturalist's
mind when we compare any of the emotionally wrought
deaths of Shakespeare's heroines—let us say Desdemona—
with the death of Zenocrate in *Tamburlaine*. To Tamburlaine's question as to how she fares, she answers:

> I fare my Lord, as other Empresses,
> That when this frail and transitory flesh
> Hath sucked the measure of that vital air
> That feeds the body with his dated health,
> Wanes with enforced and necessary change.

Such flat serenity comes only rarely to the naturalist's mind,
and then only at the prospect of yielding calmly to natural
law. More often he is angrily regarding the world with
suspicion and finding it no preparation for heaven but an
intimation of quite something else.

> Hell hath no limits, nor is circumscribed
> In one self place, for where we are is hell . . .

The naturalist cannot help compiling the detail of hell.
He can see no pattern in this detail, and indeed it is the lack
of pattern which occasions his point of view. And so he
gathers together the detail, whether or not it is repetitious,
and says: "Here it is. It is not a pretty bundle." Yet when
the burden of squalor for Marlowe becomes intolerable,
he is able to escape into a baroque sensualism, such as he
drew purely—but never again as purely—in *Hero and
Leander*. In the plays his happy reverie of sensual delights
is always presented with a flicker of cynical scorn. One remembers the hypocritical Gaveston in *Edward the Second*
informing the audience that he "must have wanton poets"

to create voluptuous pictures for the king. One remembers that it is the silly old nurse in *Dido, Queen of Carthage,* who, having fallen in love with the boy Ascanius, voices one of Marlowe's most shimmering and lovely descriptions. And one remembers that it is the depraved slave, Ithamore, in *The Jew of Malta,* who tells his courtesan:

> Content, but we will leave this paltry land,
> And sail from hence to Greece, to lovely Greece. . . .
> I'll be Adonis, thou shalt be Love's Queen.

Although Marlowe's escapist visions of epicurean happiness are linked to circumstances which infect them with sarcastic doubt, in themselves perhaps they represent Marlowe's idea of what life—or at least life on this earth—should ideally be. Nevertheless, it is precisely this romantic sensualism which Marlowe repudiates in *Doctor Faustus,* his great play. It is not easy to enucleate the reason for this, but I think it stems from his awareness of the cleavage between the humanism of the past and the naturalism of his present and the future.

Marlowe in his own time was rumored to be an "atheist." Whatever his heterodoxy, Marlowe was certainly not an atheist, although his religion could not persist by ignoring the disparity between man's behavior and the divine commitment. This is the reason for his satire of Christianity in *Tamburlaine* and *The Jew of Malta,* but it is also the reason for the sublimity of *Doctor Faustus;* for Marlowe's religious feelings could find expression only by rejecting the natural world and assuming a supernatural one, by repudiating sensuality and assuming a divine moral judgment. In denying the natural world, however, the technique of its assertion—that is, episodic detail, repetition, and ramification—remained. The method would, of course, present itself as appropriate, for if the naturalistic point of view observes inductively, the refutation of that view may logically proceed inductively. But I may be too logical here. It may be that Marlowe could not have changed his method had he wished to. At any rate, by employing the technique appropriate to naturalism in a supernatural play Marlowe came to write the most intensely religious play of the English Renaissance.

In a similar fashion Jeffers, the materialist, naturalist, and Inhumanist, came to write *The Double Axe,* one of the few profoundly religious poems of this century. Neither *Doctor Faustus* nor *The Double Axe* is, in the traditional sense, a tragedy. They are, however, the special tragedies which occur when an instinctive naturalism is brought to bay by an instinctive religiosity, and they readily take on something of the form of the morality play. In such a form there are no characters in the last analysis except the character of the author, who must, by a careful self-humiliation, bring the detail to a final hardness of meaning, a final, blunt salvation. He sacrifices, burns away the persons of his drama; but that is his privilege, for they are, like the characters in a morality play, the projections of a conflict: a conflict, however, less of theology than of the religious temperament. In understanding this, we may discard the term "morality play" and substitute the more suitable one, "debate."

Jeffers' narratives are the diary of disparate phantoms who constitute a sensibility at war with itself. Excepting *Roan Stallion,* they all take on the lineaments of an inner debate which derives its puissance from the discernment of a discrepancy between the laws of God and the laws of man. But, and *Doctor Faustus* in Marlowe's career is precedent for this, Jeffers' debate becomes the grand debate in only one work.

In retrospection it is possible to see that Jeffers' earlier long poems were working toward the consummation of *The Double Axe*. The characters, for example, are hardly ever characters; they are often psychic contestants. Closer to the matter are all the alter egos, those fracturings of consciousness. The strain of the debate itself is adumbrated by Barclay's harangues in *The Women at Point Sur* and by shorter poems like "Meditation on Saviors," where Jeffers addresses himself as "you." But these are only a modest token of the friction in the interior argument developed in *The Double Axe*:

. . . after he had considered the matter more fully, he said: "Nothing is valueless: but some things are obnoxious."
Then truly began the strain of thought. The old man paced back and forth on the hill, sweating and groaning, and at length he said humbly:
"To me."
But even so the matter was not concluded, for the old man's axe in his hand began to spit like a cat, and he stared at it and said proudly: "I agree with you. To *me*. Who has a better right to judge?
God does not judge: God *is*. Mine is the judgment."

Even the double axe—the ancient phallic symbol of reproduction and clearly also a symbol of destruction—reflects the deep-rooted contentions.

Because of these contentions, only his adaptation of the *Medea* realizes Jeffers' own aim in tragedy as "poetry . . . beautiful shapes . . . violence." And this only because of the organic simplicity that Euripides imposes on Jeffers' restive imagination—an imagination which, when free to follow its own bent, is hardly capable of producing a stageable drama. Almost everywhere else in Jeffers' poetry the contentions grind against each other, reducing human character to dust, destroying those very structures and relationships which recommend themselves as essential to narrative and dramatic success. I cheerfully concede these points to Jeffers' detractors. Nor do I wish to minimize these faults. Yet even after such a large loss, something large remains, and if we do not minimize this remainder, we see that it is poetry.

Such a strange poetry for our time. For America believes that truth and goodness are relative to temporary successes in "adjusting" the greedy claim of one group or creature to another, the lobbyist to the lobbyist, the student to the teacher; it believes, therefore, that language, morals, and intellect must adjust to adjustments within adjustments, so that no one will be made unhappy by anyone's having perfected an individual happiness. But Jeffers' poetry is wondrously maladjusted, a poetry of immense loneliness. I do not mean to imply that other poets especially sanction this salvation by adjustment. W. H. Auden, for example, satirizes the reduction of the citizen to a social security number, but the terms that Mr. Auden uses are those of the social system. The effect of his criticism is to continue an awareness of those things he decries; an awareness that certainly does not weaken the criticism and may enhance the satire. Indeed, do not the crests of satire occur when the satirist does not want to change the existing structures, only to purify them? Satire is a conservative art. The effect, however, of Jeffers' poetry is of another sort; his

poetry does not participate in the sins that it abhors. Whereas many today would have us assert a greater individuality
—would even have us adjust to a greater individuality—
Jeffers' poetry *lives* as an individuality. In short, if Jeffers'
narratives want characterizations, they do not want character.

Even as the persons of Jeffers' stories disappear upon
their impossible stage, a large, single person appears, as if
by incantation, to fill the stage with a pervading soliloquy.
Here the hawk strikes its beak against the rock. Here the
components of the lonely soul debate the sacred matters of
life and death. Here are made those decisions that can only
be made by a great effort of integrity within the recesses of
self. Among the decisions one decision stands clear: Any
imaginable corruption may be expected to develop in the
massive polyorganism of society, for society has no single
conscience; but for the individual "corruption has never
been compulsory."

No doubt future critics will argue the value of this decision, as well as Jeffers' means of expressing it. But I doubt
that any criticism will be more searching than Jeffers' own
"Self-Criticism in February," cast appropriately in the form
of a debate with himself:

> The bay is not blue but sombre yellow
> With wrack from the battered valley, it is speckled with
> violent foam-heads
> And tiger-striped with long lovely storm-shadows.
> *You love this better than the other mask; better eyes than*
> *yours*
> *Would feel the equal beauty in the blue.*
> *It is certain you have loved the beauty of storm dispropor-*
> *tionately.*

But the present time is not pastoral, but founded
On violence, pointed for more massive violence: perhaps it
   is not
Perversity but need that perceives the storm-beauty.
Well, bite on this: your poems are too full of ghosts and
   demons,
And people like phantoms—how often life's are—
And passion so strained that the clay mouths go praying
   for destruction—
Alas, it is not unusual in life;
To every soul at some time. *But why insist on it? And now*
For the worst fault: you have never mistaken
Demon nor passion nor idealism for the real God.
Then what is most disliked in those verses
Remains most true. *Unfortunately. If only you could sing*
That God is love, or perhaps that social
Justice will soon prevail. I can tell lies in prose.

X

Whitman, Lucretius, and Jeffers

1

ALTHOUGH THE ULTIMATE psychological effect of Jeffers' narratives is that of the insular soul warring within itself, it is also true that there is a public aspect to the poetry. The poetry is engaged with society to the extent that it takes up an isolated position which assaults society; it is not engaged to the extent that it enters society in order to criticize it.

Robinson Jeffers as early as 1929 wrote that he was "quits with the people,"[1] but he has in fact never been content to leave the people alone. For better or worse he has urged a constant politics, at the core of which reposes his cyclical theory of history. He deplores the extended civilization that trades spiritual power for material greatness. War, he thinks, helps to bring about this fat decadence, for the reason that it intimidates the one social value Jeffers worships—freedom. It is necessary to observe that Jeffers separates "freedom" from "democracy." For him "democracy" signifies "prosperous slavery." He supposes that democracy leads to an emphasis on a generalized prosperity which, along with war, kills freedom, and when freedom is dead the machine of society breaks down.[2]

The liaison between freedom and austerity is the stress of the trilogy of poems, "Shine, Perishing Republic" (1925), "Shine, Republic" (1935), and "Shine, Empire" (1941). In the first of these "democracy" is equated with decadence:

> While this America settles in the mould of its vulgarity, heavily thickening to empire,
> And protest, only a bubble in the molten mass, pops and sighs out, and the mass hardens,
>
> I sadly smiling remember that the flower fades to make fruit, the fruit rots to make earth.
> Out of the mother; and through the spring exultances, ripeness and decadence; and home to the mother.

Whereas "Shine, Perishing Republic" reflects the Spenglerian mood and records a resignation to an inevitable fate, "Shine, Republic" attempts to analyze the meaning of this fate and offers an admonition against luxury. Pondering the notion of ineluctable patterns, it offers advice:

> ... you, America ... You were not born to prosperity, you were born to love freedom.
> You did not say "en masse," you said "independence." But we cannot have all the luxuries and freedom also.

By 1941, however, Jeffers once more regarded the fate as sealed, the propositions inarguable, any advice empty. Another war was at hand. "Shine, Empire" describes the inescapable:

> It is war, and no man can see an end of it. We must put freedom away and stiffen into bitter empire.

> All Europe was hardly worth the precarious freedom of one
> of our states: what will her ashes fetch?

Jeffers has not taken the trouble of clarifying how to maintain liberty in a system other than democratic, but if one probes the republic-empire trilogy one finds that Jeffers is not objecting to the concept of equality but to a tendency toward unspirituality and state benevolism. Poverty, Jeffers says, is no evil, while simplicity is a positive virtue. Democracy, he feels, as it develops with the expanding state, inclines eventually toward socialism. Now, Jeffers' objection to socialism is not precisely the objection of political conservatism. In a letter to the poet James Rorty, he once wrote: "Of course as a matter of right and justice I sympathize with radicalism; and in any case I don't oppose it . . ."[3] The objection is in the Spenglerian dialectic "historical"; for socialism, as Spengler wrote, "forces itself to ignore the annihilating seriousness of its own final implications, so as to keep alive the illusion of the historical necessity of its own existence."[4]

Jeffers' concept of liberty is inevitably linked to his idealization of what he calls the "republic," the thinly settled nation whose poverty is its strength. "Freedom is poor and laborious," he notes and adds as his advice to America:

> But keep the tradition, conserve the forms, the observances,
>   keep the spot sore. Be great, carve deep your heel-marks.
> The states of the next age will no doubt remember you, and
>   edge their love of freedom with contempt of luxury.[5]

Intense, almost anarchistic personal freedom; the loose structure, the vigor and audacity of the frontier republic: these are meaningful political conditions to Jeffers. But he

believes we have passed beyond the period which produces
these as the accidents of growth. Or, as he wrote with dis-
concerting clairvoyance in 1943:

> There is no returning now.
> Two bloody summers from now (I suppose) we shall have
>   to take up the corrupting burden and curse of victory.
> We shall have to hold half the earth; we shall be sick with
>   self-disgust,
> And hated by friend and foe, and hold half the earth—or
>   let it go, and go down with it. Here is a burden
> We are not fit for. We are not like Romans and Britons—
>   natural world-rulers,
> Bullies by instinct—but we have to bear it. Who has kissed
>   Fate on the mouth, and blown out the lamp—must lie
>   with her.[6]

2

Because Robinson Jeffers has consistently rejected the
idea of an infinitely progressing America, he has generally
been considered the reversal of Whitman's "dream." Louis
Adamic was the first to make this observation,[7] but it has
been iterated by others, most importantly by F. O. Matthiessen,[8] with the effect of establishing it as the accepted position of critical scholarship. There is no point in arguing
that Jeffers' "pessimism" is not opposed to Whitman's "optimism"; yet the very obviousness of this difference between the two has tended to obscure the fact that they have
more in common than the tones of their rhetorics divulge.
And here the useless, hypothetical question is not utterly
useless. Would Whitman, had he written in the twentieth
century, have been the prophet of democratic magnilo-
quence? Or is it that in treating of Whitman and Jeffers we

treat of those who seek God by wrestling with the angel (some would say "devil") of their age?

Matthiessen described Whitman's political growth as veering "inevitably, though by no very coherent course, from individualism towards socialism."[9] Doubtless Matthiessen intended the word "socialism" to be taken in a relaxed sense. Even so, it is disturbing, for there is no indication that Whitman ever inclined toward a recognizable system of government which he considered superior to the individual or which he thought should regulate the aspirations and instincts toward a necessary social goal. The idea of some kind of progression is everywhere apparent, yes, but Whitman did not conceive it formally. He thought of progress as something quite as inarguable as his intuitions, an almost mystical inevitability. Similarly, when he spoke of "politics," it was not in terms of what might be accomplished by a normal state but "of the politics of Nature," which he felt was the only politics for "these States, / And that what is less than they must sooner or later lift off from these States."[10] I do not pretend to know exactly what Whitman meant by the politics of Nature, but I find it difficult to think that he was contemplating a very powerfully regulated system. Law, too, like politics, was for Whitman a function of Nature rather than of institutions. It was "the unshakable order of the universe forever."[11] And since law was Nature, man's relationship to it was neither formal nor social; far from being a political relationship, it was apolitical. Always the idea of "freedom from all laws or bonds except those of one's own being"[12] underlies Whitman's conception of democracy. Always it was the "idea of perfect individualism . . . that deepest tinges and gives character to the idea of the aggregate."[13]

Surely "democracy" for Whitman was closer to anarchy than to socialism. His major concern was with the individual and with an almost chaotic "natural" freedom. The form of state which most appealed to him in theory was, though for very different basic reasons, much like Jeffers' little republic, self-contained and minding its own business. It is true that Whitman believed that the future would establish the kind of state he dreamed of, and equally true that Jeffers sees this state only in the nostalgic terms of the perishing republic, but in their anarchistic advocacy of individual freedom Whitman and Jeffers overlap.

Since their ideals of freedom are similar it is not odd that Whitman's worries about America, his occasional qualms and doubts, prefigure Jeffers' attacks on luxury and effeteness. The failures, however, which Whitman with an "unshakable faith" believed ephemeral, are those failures which to Jeffers represent the losses that cannot be recouped. Whitman wrote:

Confess that to severe eyes, using the moral microscope upon humanity, a sort of dry and flat Sahara appears, these cities, crowded with petty grotesques, malformations, phantoms, playing meaningless antics.[14]

The phantoms and the antics increased after Whitman's death, and Jeffers, as idealistic in his way as Whitman, has continued to celebrate certain of the values that Whitman celebrated—liberty and the laws of Nature—by attacking what he believes to be inharmonious with them: the great city, the great empire. This does not constitute a reversal of Whitman's position.

3

The persuasion about Jeffers' pessimism and Whitman's optimism has obscured another and more significant relationship between them. Whitman reflected the enthusiasms of his time by honoring both a transcendental idealism and a scientific materialism. But he seemed incapable of bringing his materialism and idealism together in a single vision. It may be true that in the early poetry Whitman "could shuttle back and forth from materialism to idealism without troubling himself about any inconsistency."[15] Still, there is some evidence to suggest that when he wrote the "cluster" of poems in "Whispers of Heavenly Death" as a relatively young man (1860), he was both aware of and troubled by the hiatus between matter and idea. Without being able to answer, he asked: "Is only matter triumphant?"[16] In his last poems, perhaps when his physical infirmities made his "matter" drag, he seemed to worry considerably about the relationship between matter and idea, but, far from discovering any solution, he took a vengeful consolation in questioning the reality of the material world.

> A vague mist hanging 'round half the pages:
> (Sometimes how strange and clear to the soul,
> That all these solid things are indeed but apparitions, concepts, non-realities.)[17]

Confronted by apparitions, Whitman, with a greater intensity than one associates with the formal transcendentalist, wanted to be able to look "behind the ostent" where he felt "a mystic cipher waits unfolded."[18] He did not satisfy the desire. He appeared to feel that his own poetry had failed to close the schism of his age and that it had failed on the score of being written "with little or nothing of plan, art, erudition."[19] What he doubtless in part meant by "erudition" was scientific knowledge, for, he believed, "science, the final critic of all, has the casting vote for the future poetry."[20] He appeared to think that the great poet of the future would be able to compose the quarrel between idealism and materialism and would be, as he put it, "consistent with the Hegelian formulas, and consistent with modern science." Such a poet would discover the spirit in matter:

What the Roman Lucretius sought most nobly, yet all too blindly, negatively to do for his age and its successors, must be done positively by some great coming literatus, especially poet, who, while remaining fully poet, will absorb whatever science indicates, with spiritualism, and out of them, and out of his own genius, will compose the great poem of death. Then will man indeed confront Nature, and confront time and space, both with science, and *con amore,* and take his right place, prepared for life, master of fortune and misfortune. And then that which was long wanted will be supplied, and the ship that had it not before in all her voyages, will have an anchor.[21]

This is a curious statement. It is as though Whitman were writing a prophecy of the attempt which Jeffers was to make—an attempt to bring materialism and idealism, religion and science together, an attempt which meant that for the first time in the Christian era a poet was to test the face of Nature with the austere eyes of a Lucretius.

4

The immediate result of Jeffers' steeping himself in scientific studies as a young man was his excited and confident vision of scientific progress, as sure and happy as Whitman's golden reverie of America's greatness. His only reservation (which he later shifted to history and politics) was a fear of "the too-greatness of man." He reasoned: "Not uncorrupted the conqueror." But this reservation aside, Jeffers in 1916 felt that when Alaska was "peopled," his children might "even ascend to the stars."

> O race of men, not to be limited, striving
> With strength inexhaustible! Lo, this earth, this globe
> Of subduable rock, transnavigable ocean, how long
> Will it fix your minds and your hopes, insatiate children?[22]

The reverie was humanistic in the peculiarly self-conscious manner of the Victorian poets. As his interest in, and knowledge of, science grew, science itself became one of his instruments for attacking the humanistic tradition. It is not therefore very astonishing that his use of science has been attacked by humanists. I see no point in arguing against these attacks. They usually follow Yvor Winters' line and they usually give us a statement of what the humanist expects of poetry. As such they are valuable, normal, and intelligent; they are suggestive of the weaknesses of Jeffers' poetry but not of its strengths. We must seek to establish these strengths on appropriate grounds. If we are to deal with Jeffers at all we must do so by recognizing that there are aspects of his verse which, by being material-istic, are quite singular. We do not have to read Jeffers, but if we wish to read and criticize him intelligently it must be with an apparatus which applies to him, not one which applies to Robert Frost or Wallace Stevens.

The twentieth century has produced two important attempts to encompass science in poetry: the verse of Jeffers and Robert Bridges' *The Testament of Beauty* (1929). Bridges takes a very formal cognizance of Lucretius' *De Rerum Natura* and, like Lucretius, he expounds a systematic body of theory and knowledge, while Jeffers merely assumes and incorporates scientific learning. Nevertheless, *The Testament of Beauty* is, I think, rather remote from Lucretius' poem, for the viewpoint is not that of the Epicurean materialist but of the Miltonic humanist. Furthermore, Bridges conceives of Nature as a subjectively created "music" which without the human ear would have "no report."[23] The poetic advantages of the subjective viewpoint are obvious, and indisputably *The Testament of Beauty*, despite its eccentric orthography and archaisms, is a significant and, in places, a beautiful poem. But Bridges' Nature is not Lucretian.

The difference between Bridges' and Jeffers' approaches to science is one of emphasis; the emphasis, however is fundamental. As Guérard has pointed out, "Bridges' philosophy . . . is essentially an idealism based on natural foundations . . ."[24] And here is the important contrast: Jeffers' philosophy is essentially a materialism which yields from time to time to an idealism. But Jeffers wheels toward idealism only after materialism has been given its due. His unique effort is that of trying to observe (or to theorize about) the material universe as separated from human ambition. To the degree that this is so, we are dealing with what Santayana in his essay on Lucretius called a "naturalist" or a "materialist." These are Santayana's words:

Materialism, like any system of natural philosophy, carries with it no commandments and no advice. It merely describes the world, including the aspirations and consciences of mortals, and refers all to a material ground. The materialist, being a man, will not fail to have preferences, and even a conscience, of his own; but his precepts and policy will express, not the logical implications of his science, but his human instincts, as inheritance and experience may have shaped them. Any system of ethics might accordingly coexist with materialism; for if materialism declares certain things (like immortality) to be impossible, it cannot declare them to be undesirable. Nevertheless, it is not likely that a man so constituted as to embrace materialism will be so constituted as to pursue things which he considers unattainable. There is therefore a psychological, though no logical bond between materialism and a homely morality.[25]

This analysis, which Santayana urges as being essential for an understanding of Lucretius, helps to illuminate that part of Jeffers' poetry which is unabashedly materialistic. One cannot turn to traditional English poetry to find a precedent; it is necessary to reach back as far as Lucretius, and then, although finding precedent, one does not discover a tradition but the accident of a materialistic poem, *De Rerum Natura*. This is not surprising. The mind which yearns toward poetic expression is seldom empirical; the modern scientist is probably not a reader of verse. On historical grounds there is even less reason for surprise.

The conditions which provoked *De Rerum Natura*—a fissure between a spiritual stoicism and a materialistic Epicureanism—have, since the triumph of Christianity, been repeated only in the similar fissure between Christianity itself and the naturalistic science of the nineteenth and twentieth centuries. That much one can observe as a historical similarity, and it is engrossing. Yet one must also be ready to recognize the differences between the tensions of the second century B.C. and those of today. Only the broadest of these is pertinent to Jeffers' poetry; namely, that modern science has acquired a body of information about the structure of the universe which Democritus and Epicurus did not possess, and Christianity has fomented an intensity of concept and mythology which stoicism did not possess. The tension accordingly today is greater, and the pure vision of Lucretius is perhaps unattainable.

No writer born in the Christian tradition has been able completely to free himself from Christianity. Jeffers, like Nietzsche and D. H. Lawrence, continually adverts to the mythopoetic figure of Christ; he is repelled by the idea of the crucified titan, but he cannot leave the idea alone. Lucretius, however, could give himself over almost entirely to the system of Epicurus because, since its moral aims had much in common with stoicism, he was not tempted to synthesize those aims in the two systems and was left free to expound what was peculiar to Epicureanism—the materialistic vision. He could use that vision to arrive at his moral theses—reserve, control, and freedom of the mind, and since these were also implicit in stoicism, he did not have to waste himself in arguing against another system. He *did* have to argue against what he calls "religion"—the superstitions of life and death—but here he faced only abstractions, not an intense and emotional symbol such as confronted Nietzsche. Lucretius was wise enough, or fortunate enough, to leave the gods mainly alone. Nor was it the case, as John Evelyn thought, that Lucretius was "no great friend to Gods or Goddesses," but rather, that he felt they were no great friends to man. And so he did not tamper with them. Had he tried, on materialist grounds, to disprove or remove the gods, the unity of his naturalistic view would have surrendered to the same conflicts and desperations that strain the attitudes of Robinson Jeffers or of Henri Bergson. But Lucretius assumed that his own course and that of the gods were mutually exclusive. This was his advantage, for his materialism could remain pure, free, and independent. Jeffers has not taken the same course, nor actually could he have done so, but insofar as one can isolate his materialism, his "science," one may be able to come to a fuller appreciation of it by considering it in connection with Lucretius'.

5

On the brink of his collapse in 1926 the pathetic George Sterling brought to Jeffers a prose treatise which he had written for the "tough old mastodon" Theodore Dreiser. It was, Jeffers says, a "condensed" *De Rerum Natura*. Sterling destroyed the essay without publishing it, for (Jeffers tells us) he "would not speak publicly the thoughts he believed without reservation to be true, for fear they might hurt someone."[26] Sterling, who wrote thin, rainy songs as a modest toast to humanism, ironically accepted Lucretius' seemingly calm view of death and took his own life, while with compensatory irony Jeffers continued to write anti-humanistic poems and to argue against suicide.

Jeffers himself has intimated that he feels an affinity with Lucretius:

> Lucretius felt the change of the world in his time, the great republic riding to the height
> Whence every road leads downward; Plato in his time watched Athens
> Dance the down path. The future is a misted landscape, no man sees clearly, but at cyclic turns
> There is a change felt in the rhythm of events, as when an exhausted horse
> Falters and recovers, then the rhythm of the running hoofbeats is changed . . .
>
> One desires
> at such times

To gather the insights of the age summit against future
    loss, against the narrowing mind and the tyrants,
The pedants, the mystagogues, the barbarians: one builds
    poems for treasuries, time-conscious poems: Lucretius
Sings his great theory of natural origins and of wise con-
    duct; Plato smiling carves dreams, bright cells
Of incorruptible wax to hive the Greek honey.[27]

Although Jeffers draws Lucretius into alliance with Spengler here, it is apparent that he also wishes to go along with
him in science and morals. But note, the troubling presence
of the idealist Plato is here, too. There is always some
troubling presence to quarrel with Jeffers' materialism,
sometimes almost quelling it. In *The Double Axe,* for example, Hoult Gore's return from death and the triumph
of his will over his rotting body would seem a supernatural-
ism destructive of any naturalistic attitude—but not entirely destructive, for Hoult Gore's superior will power con-
quers only temporarily the tough fact of matter. The body
disintegrates remorselessly, tardily following natural law.
And for all his will power,

               ... what lay on the bed
    Was only bones and corruption of what had died
    On the far island ...

Hoult Gore demonstrates how insecure is Jeffers' materialism. Jeffers clearly believes that one cannot transcend natural law: things grow and decay and die; the natural world
is not God's laboratory for the sublimation of an immortal
soul. Yet, even as he confesses these things, he withholds
his signature. Despite his conviction that the facts of the
material universe are incontrovertible, he looks for something unseen which he would like to think virtuous. In the

structuring of Hoult Gore, Jeffers compromises by allowing the human soul to triumph—for a while—over Nature, to become—for a while—immortal.

Lucretius, however, was absolutely content with the belief that there was no immortality except for the gods. When the "colorless seeds" of matter disband, consciousness ceases, he says, and the soul, being mortal, like a drowned swimmer ceases to struggle and "straggles down the deepening waters of unconsciousness."[28] Jeffers, too, assumes an ephemeral soul; it dies, but not necessarily when the body dies. In the strange séance in "Come, Little Birds" (1941), Jeffers asks his father if death is "sleep." The father answers:

> "With a dream sometimes. But far
>   too bloodless to grieve," he said, "or gladden the
>   dreamer;
> And soon, I conjecture, even this pin's weight and echo
>   of consciousness that makes me speak to you
> Will dissolve in the stream." He smiled and rubbed his
>   gray hands together and said, "Amen. If you come
> To Endor again I shall not be present."

The dead dream on for a time. Jeffers makes his compromise with idealism or Christianity by lengthening the tether by which the consciousness is tied to the body. In this paradox of a brief immortality, one sees that Jeffers rebels against the materialism to which he subscribes. One must also conclude what he concludes of Hoult Gore's temporary triumph over death—that here is a tribute to the power of the human will.

Humanists, or at least the modern breed of humanists, have tended to believe that the materialistic standpoint must deny freedom of the will. True enough, behavioristic systems of psychology and biology have denied volition, but such a denial is not inevitable. Free will, as it happens, is a cornerstone in Lucretius' thought, the only way that he can explain human behavior. And one need only consider the injunction of Jeffers' Inhumanism, the injunction to turn voluntarily from passion, to realize that whatever claims matter has upon man, his will, according to Jeffers, remains free. The will depends upon the body for its existence, but even though it is responsible to matter and inseparable from it, it transcends matter in its ability to recognize and evaluate alternatives. Jeffers' narratives proceed on the grounds of an emancipated will, and while he may essay to describe the biochemical storms which surround, let us say, the emotions of love or anger, these storms do not of necessity supersede the will. When Fera Cawdor endeavors to seduce her stepson Hood, his instincts, his "chemistry" urge complicity, but he plunges his knife into his thigh, destroying lust with pain, so that even though he fights matter with matter, he does so by choice.

6

The scientific point of view has sometimes led Jeffers into absurdities of language ("autolytic enzymes"), but it has also led him to very unique beauties. The humanistic point of view is adapted to describing man and is the superior view for this purpose, but the materialist's attitude is better for describing Nature as the landscape—not of man —but of God. The humanist supposes that what pleases the good man pleases God. The Lucretian poet, having no reason to believe that what pleases him also pleases God, is released into a consideration of the immensity and the omnipotence of Nature. The release may in some ways be harrowing and comfortless, yet it seems to me that no poet in the humanist tradition approaches the spare grandeur of Lucretius when he describes the emergence of earth from chaos, the gigantic birth attended by a choir of indestructible particles of matter, the myriad, insectile gleams of the atoms swirling through the primeval ether. And it seems to me that Jeffers alone among contemporaries, and better perhaps than any poet since Lucretius, attains a released vision of Nature. Sometimes it occurs in poems of "constructed" reality; that is to say, in poems where the imagination attempts to penetrate beyond what can be "seen" in Nature, as Lucretius attempted to "perceive" a universe of atoms. In this spirit Jeffers writes:

> Sleep deepened over him
> Like heavy ocean, more like coma than sleep; his mind
> made no appreciable dreams,
> But crawling blindly about his body like a numbed spider
> on its web of nerves, here it shook a filament,
> There a dark ganglion faintly glowed for a moment and
> returned to darkness, a pin-point nexus of brain-
> cells
> Grew phosphorescent and faded and faintly glowed
> again . . . [29]

Here the human body is related to the pattern of the greater universe; this passage might be the description of a paroxysm in a galaxy, or of the dance in the atom; it places man precisely in the central position which science tells us he occupies in the universe, midway in mass between the atom and the largest star. Does this dwarf man or magnify him? The question has little importance for a materialist. But even for the humanist, it seems to me, Jeffers offers a vision of human participation in magnificence.

The humanist is apt to see science as an arrogant agent bent on destroying God and religion. For the materialist, however, the opposite is true. Because he assumes that the ultimate reality is a supremely ordered matter, the materialist thinks of science as a way of observing the order, as a devotion, a religion. (The irony of all this is that science only becomes arrogant or dangerous when it gets into the hands of humanists who try to use it for human gain or "progress.") The tones of devotion in Jeffers' descriptions of Nature reveal the sacramental signification of science for him. He scoffs at applied science in his poem on Edison. He suggests how scientific knowledge may lead to perversity in "Margrave" and in *Such Counsels You Gave to Me,* where "scientists" in their pursuit of natural knowledge cease to be natural. Losing balance, they destroy what is natural. Jeffers does not tempt us toward this imbalance; he asks us to believe that science is properly "an adoration; a kind of worship."[30] Like Blake, he sees a sacred vision in the sun:

> "Holy, holy, holy,"
> Sing the angels of the sun, pouring out power
> On the lands and the planets . . .[31]

One suspects that the young Jeffers turned to the study of science in order to destroy the religion of his father. If so, it is ironically appropriate that science should become the handmaiden of his own religion. One must once again observe how impossible it has been for Jeffers to achieve the purely materialistic point of view. Even so, he and Lucretius are parallel in one fundamental way. They both write

the poem of death which at the same time is the poem of
God.

The materialist, Lucretius, and the semimaterialist, Jeffers, argue against the fear of death. Yet we may wonder if
the reason that such minds embrace materialism is not
partly that they have, to begin with, an *extraordinary* aver-
sion to dying. Most men naturally dislike the idea of death,
but usually because they love life rather than because they
fear death. A man, or rather let us specify a poet, haunted
by a fear of death might try to whisper himself free of that
fear by turning his gaze toward the recurring spectacle of
death—that is, to Nature itself. So gazing, he would then
be able to assure himself that death comes and goes, that it
is the most common of phenomena, and that death itself
is a necessary part of re-creation.

Whether or not such a psychological defense, a numb-
ing by satiation, stands behind Lucretius' and Jeffers' contemplation of the panorama of deaths, from such a contemplation comes a profound reaction. The materialist's
long reading of the repeated canto of mutability in Nature's
book seems reflected in his impression of God. Just as the
humanist demands perfection, freedom from caprice in
his God, so too, does the materialist; and yet, since the materialist's attention is fixed upon the spectacle of death, he
tends to remove God entirely away from that very matter
which he claims to be the essence of all things. Lucretius is
most vague about the composition of the gods. He insists
that they are material, yet he qualifies the materialism with
the word *tenuis* (subtle). The gods are immortal, he appears to think, not because their material is immortal but
because their forms do not change. Interpretation is diffi-

cult here, but this would seem to mean that the gods do not possess a "numerical" atomic reality but a permanence, an immortality of renewable form, an eternal magnetism to which the atomic pilgrims are drawn again and again. Most significantly, however, Lucretius, following Epicurus, supposes that the gods dwell in the "spaces between the worlds":[32] that is to say, they dwell in the void. But does this not mean that they are ultimately to be dissociated from the character of matter and from the constant warfare of death and life, creation and destruction?

Jeffers' God is not so difficult to find as Lucretius' gods, but that God must be separable from Nature itself seems implicit in Jeffers' telling us of the spirit of God that:

> The spirit (to call it so: what else could I call it?) is not
> a personal quality, and not
> Mortal; it comes and goes, never dies. It is not to be found
> in death: dredge not the shadow-world.[33]

God, then, "comes and goes," renewing himself infinitely, but if he "is not to be found in death," then Jeffers' conception of God is separate from his view of Nature; then Jeffers' conception of God is not finally pantheistic, even though for most purposes it is convenient and proper so to describe it. In the pinches, his God retreats from Nature, from death, and becomes a "spirit," hidden in the interstellar, or perhaps interatomic, spaces where the Epicurean gods reposed. This conception might underlie the symbolical implications of Jeffers' use of the word "desert." The desert in verse of the romantic tradition often symbolizes spiritual drought or the absence of God, a symbol which comes to perfection in *The Waste Land*. Jeffers' symbolic use of the desert runs counter to this tendency, and one is tempted to believe that if his God escapes the limitations of matter, which constrain all else, by dwelling in emptiness, it is appropriate that the desert should emerge as the symbol not of spiritual drought but of spiritual fullness. The phrase "desert of the spirit occurs more than once in the poetry, and in the lyric, "The Soul's Desert," he writes:

> Clearly it is time
> To become disillusioned, each person to enter his own soul's
>   desert
> And look for God—having seen man.

The "soul's desert" is the password to peace, but by reason of the idealist dilution of his materialism Jeffers has never been able to achieve the profoundly sane and dignified peace which appears to have come effortlessly to Lucretius. Only after burning and humiliation can Jeffers find God in the desert. But what the reader of poetry, or the reader who is interested in the destiny of man, can discover is that in Jeffers' work the first major poetic attempt to bring the split of the modern world together in a primarily materialistic vision has been made.

I have a final observation. The future history of culture would be a chronicle of cowardice, should man shy utterly away from the challenge which science has laid down. Poetry's learning can never afford to be very different from society's. Man and his art must get along with the knowledge which temporal experience provides and, indeed, imposes. And poetry could never again claim ripeness, should it insist that it can only see beauty and truth by holding its hands over its eyes. Jeffers has asked us to look squarely at the universe. He has told us that materialism has its message, its relevance, and its solace. These are different from the message, relevance, and solace of human-ism. Humanism teaches us best *why* we suffer, but material-ism (and Whitman would have appreciated this, perhaps intended this in referring to "the great poem of death") teaches us best *how* to suffer.

NOTES

Introduction

1. *Robinson Jeffers, the Man and the Artist* (New York, 1926), pp. 25–39.
2. In *Robinson Jeffers, an Artist,* ed. John S. Mayfield (1928), pages unnumbered.
3. James Daly, "Roots under the Rocks," *Poetry: A Magazine of Verse,* August, 1925, p. 280.
4. *The Liberation of American Literature* (1932), p. 474.
5. *American Mirror* (1940), pp. 268–69.
6. *Time,* October 18, 1937, p. 87.
7. "The Dilemma of Robinson Jeffers," *Poetry,* March, 1934, pp. 338–42.
8. "Jeffers on the Age," *Poetry,* February, 1937, p. 280.
9. "Science and the Poetry of Robinson Jeffers," *American Literature,* X (November, 1938), p. 285.
10. "Sources of Violence," *Poetry,* October, 1939, p. 38.
11. See *In Defense of Reason* (New York, 1947), pp. 30–35.
12. R. P. Blackmur, "Lord Tennyson's Scissors: 1912–1950," *The Kenyon Review,* Winter, 1952, p. 11.
13. John Crowe Ransom, "The Poetry of 1900 1950," *The Kenyon Review,* Summer, 1951, pp. 445–54.
14. Horace Gregory and Marya Zaturenska, *American Poetry 1900–1940* (New York, 1946), p. 407.
15. Ned Rosenheim, "One Tiger on the Road," *Poetry,* March, 1949, p. 353.
16. Louise Bogan, *Achievement in American Poetry 1900–1950* (New York, 1951), p. 77.

I

1. Lawrence C. Powell, *Robinson Jeffers, the Man and His Work* (Pasadena, 1940), p. 7.
2. S. S. Alberts, *A Bibliography of the Works of Robinson Jeffers* (New York, 1933), pp. xv–xvi.

3. Lawrence C. Powell, *op. cit.,* p. 10.

4. *Ibid.,* p. 14.

5. Melba Berry Bennett, *Robinson Jeffers and the Sea* (San Francisco, 1936), pp. 17–18.

6. *The Selected Poetry of Robinson Jeffers* (New York, 1938), pp. xv–xvi.

7. Letter to Lawrence Clark Powell. Powell, *op. cit.,* p. 17.

8. *Ibid.,* p. xvii.

9. Letter of Miss Laura E. Burmeister to Lawrence Clark Powell. *Ibid.,* p. 12.

10. Edith Greenan, *Of Una Jeffers* (Los Angeles, 1939), p. 8.

11. See Alberts, *op. cit.,* p. 154.

12. *Ibid.*

13. Greenan, *op. cit.,* pp. 9–10, 35.

14. Horace Gregory and Marya Zaturenska, *American Poetry 1900–1940* (1946), pp. 405–6.

15. Alberts, *op. cit.,* pp. 37–38.

16. *The Double Axe and Other Poems* (New York, 1948), p. vii.

II

1. *The Concept of Nature in Nineteenth Century Poetry* (1936), p. 543.

2. *The Double Axe and Other Poems* (New York, 1948), p. 113.

3. *Ibid.,* p. 56.

4. Eric Bentley, *The Cult of the Superman* (London, 1947), p. 227.

5. Friedrich W. Nietzsche, *Beyond Good and Evil,* trans. Helen Zimmern, pp. 386–87. In *The Philosophy of Nietzsche* (New York: The Modern Library, 1937. Revised pagination). All subsequent citations of Nietzsche refer to this edition.

6. *Solstice and Other Poems* (New York, 1935), p. 1.

7. *The Selected Poetry of Robinson Jeffers* (New York, 1938), p. xviii.

8. *Beyond Good and Evil,* p. 435.

9. Nietzsche, *Thus Spake Zarathustra,* trans. Thomas Common, p. 91.

10. "Why I Am So Wise," *Ecce Homo,* trans. Clifton P. Fadiman, p. 827.

11. Letter (January, 1938) to Frederic I. Carpenter. In Carpenter, "The Values of Robinson Jeffers," *American Literature*, XI (January, 1940), p. 366.

12. "Why I Am So Wise," *Ecce Homo*, p. 824.

13. Arthur Schopenhauer, *The World as Will and Idea*, trans. R. B. Haldane and J. Kemp, p. 202. In *The Works of Schopenhauer*, ed. Will Durant (1931). Subsequent citations of Schopenhauer refer to this edition.

14. "The Answer," *Selected Poetry*, p. 594.

15. *The World as Will and Idea*, p. 5.

16. Schopenhauer, "The Ages of Life," *Essays*, trans. T. Bailey Saunders, pp. 413–14.

17. *The World as Will and Idea*, p. 268.

18. *Ibid.*, pp. 144–45.

III

1. Oswald Spengler, *The Decline of the West*, ed., trans. Charles F. Atkinson (New York, 1950), I, p. 94.

2. *Ibid.*, I, p. 151.

3. *Ibid.*, II, p. 3

4. *Ibid.*, I, pp. 106–7.

5. *Ibid.*, I, p. 352.

6. *Ibid.*, I, p. 108.

7. *Ibid.*, II, pp. 103–4.

8. *The Double Axe and Other Poems* (New York, 1948), p. 81.

9. Spengler, *op. cit.*, I, pp. 142–43.

10. *Ibid.*, I, p. 168.

11. Robinson Jeffers, *Poetry, Gongorism and a Thousand Years* (Los Angeles, 1949), pp. 4, 9.

12. Spengler, *op. cit.*, pp. 93–94.

IV

1. See John S. Mayfield, *Robinson Jeffers, an Artist* (Dallas, 1928).

2. Havelock Ellis, *Psychology of Sex* (New York, 1938), p. 361.

3. *Fountain of Life* (Boston and New York, 1930), p. 385.

4. "Orca," *The Double Axe and Other Poems* (New York, 1948), p. 144.

5. Lawrence C. Powell, *Robinson Jeffers, the Man and His Work* (Pasadena, 1940), p. 40.

6. *Ibid.*, p. 41.

7. Carl Jung, *Collected Papers on Analytical Psychology* (1922), p. xvi.

8. *The Integration of the Personality* (New York, Toronto, 1939), p. 24.

9. *Ibid.*, p. 80.

V

1. James G. Southworth, *Some Modern American Poets* (Oxford, 1950), p. 120.

2. William Butler Yeats, *Autobiographies* (New York, 1927), p. 353.

3. H. H. Waggoner, "Science and the Poetry of Robinson Jeffers," *American Literature*, X (November, 1938), p. 287.

4. Lawrence C. Powell, *Robinson Jeffers, the Man and His Work* (Pasadena, 1940), p. 6.

5. Hildegarde Flanner, "Two Poets: Jeffers and Millay," *The New Republic*, January 27, 1937, p. 380.

6. "Meditation on Saviors," *The Selected Poetry of Robinson Jeffers* (New York, 1938), pp. 200–204.

7. See *The Spiritual Aspects of the New Poetry* (1940), p. 147.

8. *Shine, Perishing Republic; Robinson Jeffers and the Tragic Sense in Modern Poetry* (Boston, 1936), p. 50.

9. "Going to Horse Flats," *Such Counsels You Gave to Me and Other Poems* (New York, 1937), pp. 90–91.

10. *The Double Axe and Other Poems* (New York, 1948), p. 68.

11. *Ibid.*, pp. 53–54.

VI

1. *In Defense of Reason* (New York, 1947), p. 93.

2. S. S. Alberts, *A Bibliography of the Works of Robinson Jeffers* (New York, 1933), p. 110.

3. *Lorenzo in Taos* (London, 1932), p. 15.

4. Lawrence C. Powell, *Robinson Jeffers, the Man and His Work* (Pasadena, 1940), pp. 58–59. See also Harry T. Moore, *The Life and Works of D. H. Lawrence* (New York, 1951), p. 225.

5. D. H. Lawrence, *St. Mawr* (Penguin Books, 1950), p. 78.

6. "Self-Criticism in February," *The Selected Poetry of Robinson Jeffers* (New York, 1938), p. 601.

7. *Fantasia of the Unconscious* (New York, 1922), pp. 266–67.

8. *Ibid.*, p. 163.

9. Powell, *op. cit.*, p. 20.

10. D. H. Lawrence, *Fire and Other Poems* (1930), pp. v–vii.

11. "New Mexico Mountains," *Selected Poetry*, p. 363.

12. Alberts, *op. cit.*, p. 111.

13. See Frajam Taylor, "The Hawk and the Stone," *Poetry: A Magazine of Verse*, October, 1939, pp. 39–46.

VII

1. "Air-Raid Rehearsals," *Such Counsels You Gave to Me and Other Poems* (New York, 1937), p. 101.

2. *The Smart Set*, August, 1913, pp. 117–18.

3. "Meditation on Saviors," *The Selected Poetry of Robinson Jeffers* (New York, 1938), pp. 200, 204.

4. "The Answer," *ibid.*, p. 594.

5. "Mara," *Be Angry at the Sun* (New York, 1941), p. 67.

6. *The Double Axe and Other Poems* (New York, 1948), pp. 56–57.

7. *Ibid.*, p. 83.

8. *Such Counsels You Gave to Me*, p. 72.

9. "Going to Horse Flats," *ibid.*, pp. 90–91.

10. "Boats in a Fog," *Selected Poetry*, p. 163.

11. "Now Returned Home," *ibid.*, pp. 612–13.

12. *The Double Axe*, p. vii.

13. "What Are Cities for?" *Selected Poetry*, p. 566.

14. "The Excesses of God," *Be Angry at the Sun*, p. 104.

15. *The Double Axe*, p. 106.

VIII

1. "Cassandra," *The Double Axe and Other Poems* (New York, 1948), p. 117.

2. "The Great Sunset," *The Selected Poetry of Robinson Jeffers* (New York, 1938), p. 591.

3. "My Dear Love," *Be Angry at the Sun* (New York, 1941), pp. 107–8.

4. "Shine, Empire," *ibid.*, p. 150.

5. "The Tower Beyond Tragedy," *Selected Poetry*, pp. 118–19.

6. *Selected Poetry*, p. xiv.

7. "Fire," *Hungerfield and Other Poems* (New York, 1954), p. 103.

8. "The Hellenism of Robinson Jeffers," *The Kenyon Critics*, ed. John Crowe Ransom (Cleveland, 1951), p. 310.

9. *Selected Poetry*, p. xv.

10. *Poetry, Gongorism and a Thousand Years* (Los Angeles, 1949), pp. 4–5.

IX

1. Letter to Jake Zeitlin (March 22, 1935) in *Robinson Jeffers, 1905–1935*, comp. Lawrence Clark Powell, 1935, pages unnumbered.

2. *The Double Axe and Other Poems* (New York, 1948), p. 95.

3. S. S. Alberts, *A Bibliography of the Works of Robinson Jeffers* (New York, 1933), p. 110.

4. *Poetry, Gongorism and a Thousand Years* (Los Angeles, 1949), p. 8.

5. *In Defense of Reason* (New York, 1947), pp. 32, 34.

6. *The New Criticism* (Norfolk, Conn., 1941), pp. 236–37.

7. Allen Tate and Frances Cheney, *Sixty American Poets* (Washington, 1945), p. 64.

8. *In Defense of Reason*, p. 34.

9. *The Spiritual Aspects of the New Poetry*, p. 144.

X

1. "Birth-Dues," *The Selected Poetry of Robinson Jeffers* (New York, 1938), p. 262.

2. See "Hellenistics," *Selected Poetry*, p. 603.

3. S. S. Alberts, *A Bibliography of the Works of Robinson Jeffers* (New York, 1933), p. 39.

4. Oswald Spengler, *The Decline of the West* (New York, 1950), I, p. 364.

5. "Shine Republic," *Selected Poetry*, p. 568.

6. "Historical Choice," *The Double Axe and Other Poems* (New York, 1948), p. 129.

7. Louis Adamic, *Robinson Jeffers, a Portrait* (Seattle, 1929), pp. 34–35.

8. *American Renaissance* (London and New York, 1941), pp. 592–93.

9. *Ibid.*, p. 543.

10. *Leaves of Grass* in *The Complete Poetry and Prose of Walt Whitman,* ed. Malcolm Cowley (Garden City, New York, 1948), I, p. 257. Subsequent citations refer to this edition.

11. *Democratic Vistas,* II, p. 223.

12. *Ibid.*, p. 247.

13. *Ibid.*, p. 218.

14. *Ibid.*, p. 216.

15. *American Renaissance,* p. 521.

16. *Leaves of Grass,* I, p. 389.

17. *Ibid.*, p. 456.

18. *Ibid.*

19. *Good-Bye My Fancy,* II, pp. 537–38.

20. *Ibid.*, p. 511.

21. *Democratic Vistas,* II, p. 255.

22. "Dream of the Future," *Californians* (New York, 1916), p. 175.

23. *The Testament of Beauty,* I, p. 82.

24. Albert Joseph Guérard, Jr., *Robert Bridges* (Cambridge, Mass., 1942), p. 186.

25. George Santayana, *Three Philosophical Poets* (Cambridge, 1927), pp. 32–33.

26. Alberts, *op. cit.,* p. 136.

27. "Prescription of Painful Ends," *Be Angry at the Sun* (New York, 1941), pp. 101–2.

28. *De Rerum Natura,* ed., trans. Cyril Bailey (London and New York, 1947), III, p. 829.

29. *Such Counsels You Gave to Me and Other Poems* (New York, 1937), p. 17.

30. *The Double Axe,* p. 92.

31. "Fire," *Hungerfield and Other Poems* (New York, 1954), p. 103.

32. *De Rerum Natura.* See Bailey's Introduction, I, pp. 68–69.

33. "Come Little Birds," *Be Angry at the Sun* (New York, 1941), p. 118.

Bibliography

Works by [John] Robinson Jeffers

Flagons and Apples. Los Angeles: Grafton Publishing Company, 1912.

"Mirrors," *The Smart Set,* XL:4 (1913), 117–18.

Californians. New York: The Macmillan Company, 1916.

Tamar and Other Poems. New York: Peter G. Boyle, 1924.

Roan Stallion, Tamar and Other Poems. New York: Boni and Liveright, 1925. New York: The Modern Library, 1935.

The Women at Point Sur. New York: Horace Liveright, 1927.

An Artist. Dallas: John S. Mayfield, 1928.

Cawdor and Other Poems. New York: Horace Liveright, 1928.

Poems. San Francisco: The Book Club of California, 1928.

Dear Judas, and Other Poems. New York: Horace Liveright, 1929.

Apology for Bad Dreams. Paris: Harry Ward Ritchie, 1930.

Stars. Pasadena: The Flame Press, 1930.

Descent to the Dead, Poems Written in Ireland and Great Britain. New York: Random House, 1931.

Thurso's Landing and Other Poems. New York: Liveright, Inc., 1932.

Give Your Heart to the Hawks and Other Poems. New York: Random House, 1933.

Return. San Francisco: Gelber, Lilienthal, Inc., 1934.

Rock and Hawk. New Haven: Frederic Prokosch, 1934.

Four Poems and a Fragment. Copyright edition. Yonkers: S. S. Alberts, 1935.

Solstice and Other Poems. New York: Random House, 1935.

The Beaks of Eagles. San Francisco: The Grabhorn Press for Albert M. Bender, 1936.

Hope Is Not for the Wise. San Mateo: The Quercus Press, 1937.

Such Counsels You Gave to Me and Other Poems. New York: Random House, 1937.

Poems Known and Unknown. Copyright edition. Yonkers: S. S. Alberts, 1938.

The Selected Poetry of Robinson Jeffers. New York: Random House, 1938.

The House-Dog's Grave. San Mateo: The Quercus Press, 1939.

Be Angry at the Sun. New York: Random House, 1941.

Medea, Freely Adapted from the Medea of Euripides. New York: Random House, 1946.

The Double Axe and Other Poems. New York: Random House, 1948.

Poetry, Gongorism and a Thousand Years. Reprinted from *The New York Times* (Jan. 18, 1948). Los Angeles: Ward Ritchie Press, 1949.

Hungerfield and Other Poems. New York: Random House, 1954.

The Tower Beyond Tragedy, Adapted by Robinson Jeffers from His Poem, The Tower Beyond Tragedy. Acting version. New York: The American National Theatre and Academy (no date).

Books and Articles on Jeffers

ADAMIC, LOUIS, *Robinson Jeffers, a Portrait.* Seattle: University of Washington Bookstore, 1929. 35 pp.

ALBERTS, S. S., *A Bibliography of the Works of Robinson Jeffers.* New York: Random House, 1933.

BENNETT, MELBA B., *Robinson Jeffers and the Sea.* San Francisco: Gelber, Lilienthal, Inc., 1936.

"California Hybrid," *Time,* XXX (October 18, 1937), 86–87.

CARPENTER, FREDERIC I., "Death Comes for Robinson Jeffers," *University Review,* VII (1941), 97–105.

——, "The Values of Robinson Jeffers," *American Literature,* XI (1940), 353–66.

Cestre, Charles, "Robinson Jeffers," *Revue Anglo-Américaine,* IV (1927), 489–502.

Daly, James, "Roots under the Rocks," *Poetry,* XXVI (1925), 278–85.

Davis, Harold L., "Jeffers Denies Us Twice," *Poetry,* XXXI (1928), 274–79.

Deutsch, Babette, "Brains and Lyrics," *The New Republic,* XLIII:547 (1925), 23–24.

Flanner, Hildegarde, "Two Poets: Jeffers and Millay," *The New Republic,* LXXXIX:1156 (1937), 379–82.

Fletcher, John G., "The Dilemma of Robinson Jeffers," *Poetry,* XLIII (1934), 338–42.

Flint, F. S., "Recent Verse," *Criterion* (London), VIII (1928), 342–46.

Gierasch, Walter, "Robinson Jeffers," *English Journal,* XXVIII (1939), 284–95.

Gilbert, Rudolph, *Shine, Perishing Republic; Robinson Jeffers and the Tragic Sense in Modern Poetry.* Boston: Bruce Humphries, Inc., 1936.

Greenan, Edith, *Of Una Jeffers.* Los Angeles: Ward Ritchie Press, 1939.

Humphries, Rolfe, "Robinson Jeffers," *Modern Monthly,* VIII (1935), 680–89.

Johnson, William S., "The Savior in the Poetry of Robinson Jeffers," *American Literature,* XV (1943), 159–68.

Morris, Lloyd S., "Robinson Jeffers: The Tragedy of a Modern Mystic," *The New Republic,* LIV (1928), 386–90.

Powell, Lawrence Clark, *An Introduction to Robinson Jeffers.* Dijon: Imprimerie Bernigaud and Privat, 1932.

——, *Robinson Jeffers, the Man and His Work.* Los Angeles: The Primavera Press, 1934.

——, *Robinson Jeffers, the Man and His Work.* Pasadena: San Pasqual Press, 1940.

——, *Robinson Jeffers 1905–1935* [catalogue of]; *an Exhibition Commemorating the Thirtieth Anniversary of His Graduation from Occidental College.* Los Angeles: Ward Ritchie, 1935.

" 'Robinson Jeffers,' " *Time,* XXXII (December 26, 1938), 41.

Rorty, James, "In Major Mold," New York *Herald-Tribune* (March 1, 1925): Books, pp. 1–2.

ROSENHEIM, NED, "One Tiger on the Road," *Poetry*, LXXIII (1949), 351–54.

SCHWARTZ, DELMORE, "Sources of Violence," *Poetry*, LV (1939), 30–38.

SHORT, R. W., "The Tower Beyond Tragedy," *Southern Review*, VII (1941), 132–44.

STERLING, GEORGE, *Robinson Jeffers, the Man and the Artist*. New York: Boni and Liveright, 1926. 40 pp.

TAYLOR, FRAJAM, "The Hawk and the Stone," *Poetry*, LV (1939), 39–46.

VAN DOREN, MARK, "First Glance," *The Nation* (March 11, 1925), CXX:3114, 268.

VAN WYCK, WILLIAM, *Robinson Jeffers*. Los Angeles: Ward Ritchie Press, 1938. 17 pp.

WAGGONER, HYATT H., "Science and the Poetry of Robinson Jeffers," *American Literature*, X (1938), 276–88.

WALTON, EDA LOU, "Beauty of Storm Disproportionally," *Poetry*, LI (1938), 209–13.

WANN, LOUIS, "Robinson Jeffers: Counterpart of Walt Whitman," *Personalist*, XIX (1938), 297–308.

WARREN, ROBERT PENN, "Jeffers on the Age," *Poetry*, XLIX (1937), 279–82.

WATTS, HAROLD H., "Robinson Jeffers and Eating the Serpent," *Sewanee Review*, XLIX (1941), 39–55.

WHITE, WILLIAM, "On Some Unnoticed Jeffers Poems," *Papers, Bibliographical Society of America*, XXXIV (1940), 362–63.

WRONECKI, JEANNE, "Un Poète Américain d'Aujourd'hui: Robinson Jeffers," *Revue de France*, II (1939), 282–86.

ZABEL, MORTON D., "The Problem of Tragedy," *Poetry*, XXXII (1929), 336–40.